Jesus'
Twin

Jesus' Twin

A Dialogue WITH THE Gospel of Thomas

JAMES W. HEISIG

A Crossroad Book
The Crossroad Publishing Company
www.crossroadpublishing.com

Original title: *El gemelo de Jesús: Un alumbramiento al budismo*

The Crossroad Publishing Company
www.crossroadpublishing.com

Library of Congress Cataloging-in-Publication Data available from the Library of Congress.

ISBN: 978-0-8245-2031-1

Cover design by: George Foster
Book design by: James W. Heisig

Books published by The Crossroad Publishing Company may be purchased at special quantity discount rates for classes and institutional use. For information, please email sales@crossroadpublishing.com.

Printed in the United States of America 2015

CONTENTS

Preface

THE FIRST TIME I came upon the *Gospel of Thomas,*
over twenty years ago in the course of preparing a graduate
seminar on hermetic writings, I knew at once I was in the presence of something extraordinary. I collected what material I
could on the text in order to familiarize myself with the current state of scholarship, and then set out to read it, line by
line, with my students. Perhaps because of the year we had
given to studying reading Manichean, Mandaean, Valentinian
texts, perhaps because many of them had been raised in Buddhist families, perhaps even because of their native Japanese
religious sensitivities—for whatever reason, they felt a sponta-
neous sympathy for this collection of "secret sayings" of Jesus.

A year later I had the occasion to read the text with a group
of persons from the general public, only one of whom was
Christian. Once again, their enthusiasm for the text surprised
me. What we found together in the text made me question the
dominant view of scholars that *Thomas* stood on the gnostic
foundations of a dualism between good and evil, a rejection
of the body as inherently corrupting, and a commitment to
establishing a community of elite enlightened ones. The little
that existed in Japanese on the subject followed this same line
of thought. Unhappy with what I had read, I set to writing

a lengthy essay trying to show that not only did *Thomas* not share in this gnostic worldview, it actually advanced a restoration of the senses as an integral part of self-understanding. Ten years passed before I took up the *Gospel* again with a new group of students. In the course of our discussions it became clear that there was much more to the text than I had earlier thought. Unhappy with what I had written, I set out to collect a more extensive library of materials and to catch up with scholarly advances in the field. As enlightening as all this was, I found myself once more unhappy with what I was reading and therefore I decided to write an extensive commentary of my own. The results are the little book you now have in your hands.

I am convinced, as these pages will show, that the reasons for excluding the *Gospel of Thomas* from the Christian tradition are largely meaningless for us today. After more than half a century of concerted dialogue with other traditions, we are in a better position to recognize that not every *alter* Jesus is a Jesus *alius*. At the same time, attention to the spiritual demands being made on Christianity by our present age helps draw us more deeply into the text itself and control the tendency to immunize ourselves against its discomforts, whether through the distractions of scholarly disputation or the preoccupation with preserving orthodoxy.

I am grateful to Dean Victor Martínez and Professor Gabriel Suárez for arranging an invitation to conduct an open seminar in the theological faculty of the Universidad Javeriana of Bogotá, during which I used the text as the background to a comparison between Christian mystical thought and Buddhist ideas of the awakened self. These lectures formed the basis of the original book *El gemelo de Jesús* (Barcelona: Herder Editorial, 2006), of which this is the English translation with only minor changes.

My special thanks go to Gustavo Castaño for inviting me to live in his house, where I found the perfect blend of solitude and companionship to complete this book; and to the staff of the Nanzan Institute for Religion and Culture for their comments and suggestions.

Nagoya, Japan
1 October 2006

Profanum

Studying the text

As CHILDREN of our times, we need to take care not to rush into the sacred precincts, the *fanum,* of the text of the *Gospel of Thomas* without first taking into consideration its place in the outer precincts of current scholarship, the *profanum* of the text. Without it, we risk the sacrilege of reading too much into it and taking too little out of it—in other words, of reducing it to a fashion event that glitters in the imagination for a moment only to be replaced by something more novel. The sheer volume of historical research compiled on the text over the past forty-five years and the fervor of academic debate that has surrounded it resist easy summary. Nearly everything that follows needs some qualification, even as the views I have chosen to ignore in most cases merit the courtesy of more detailed argument than I shall supply. My aim is simpler: to frame the range of questions that occupy scholars concerning the history and composition of the text, and in this way to clarify the standpoint from which I will attempt to read it. Only when that reading has been completed will we be in a position to ask the question that these preliminary remarks are bound to provoke again and again, namely, where to place the *Gospel of Thomas* in the Christian tradition and in the wider religious inheritance of humanity.

A VOICE FROM OUTSIDE THE TRADITION

The Jesus of the *Gospel of Thomas* is unlike any other in Christian scriptures or theology. Initial speculations after the rediscovery and publication of the text in 1959 confirmed the criticisms that had circulated already from the third century, identifying him as little more than a mouthpiece for gnostic Christianity. As further study began to question the gnostic character of the *Gospel*, voices on the fringe of the scholarly activity stepped up to suggest the Jesus of the *Gospel of Thomas* was more like a Hindu or Buddhist sage, a Sufi master, or even a Cabbalist.[1] The dust his figure has kicked up in the Christian world has yet to settle,[2] but one thing is already clear: there is no easy way to graft it on to any of the variety of images of Jesus that have dominated Christian tradition down the centuries.

The blend of mythic and historical details about the life and death of Jesus recorded in the Apostolic Creed of the second century[3]—and all traces of the metaphysical language added to the Nicene Creed in the fourth century—are missing from the *Gospel of Thomas*, as is any reference to his baptism, temptation, and healings found in the four canonical gospels. There are no evil spirits menacing humanity and no demons to be cast out; there is not so much as a heaven and a hell. In fact, Jesus is not even a teacher of supernatural verities in the sense that the four gospels present him.[4] His is more the voice of an oracle than that of a preacher of selfless love and care for the poor, the hungry, the sick, and the outcast. His sayings offer no divine truths, make no prophecies, construct no philosophical arguments, and solicit no disciples. He is not presented as a redeemer or justifier of sinful humanity. No mention is made of his death, let alone of a resurrection or ascension. There is no hint of an impending apocalypse or of a return to judge the world in the final days. In effect, the historical person of Jesus is all but transparent to the reader of the text, as if to allow the words, the words of the "living Jesus," to resound with greater clarity.

The image of the human condition we meet in the *Gospel of Thomas* is also a radical departure from the scriptural and theological tradition as Christians have known it. If the language of redemption is absent, it is because human beings are not seen as born into a state of sinful disobedience which only an otherworldly divinity can rectify, but as suffering from a darkened awareness, a fundamental failure of insight into what it is that lies asleep in the recesses of their own nature.[5] There is no personal relationship of the individual with God, and indeed the idea of a transcendent creator who rules a world beyond where the rewards of heaven or the punishments of hell await us is altogether foreign to the spirit of the text.

All of this would appear to nail shut the case for rejection of the text as non-Christian. But when one begins to look at what the text actually says and to reconstruct the history of its composition, the grounds for dismissing it are less sure.

The first thing one notices skimming through *Thomas* is that it is strangely familiar. In fact, all but 20 of its 114 sayings include sentences and phrases that have parallels in the canonically accepted New Testament.[6] True, the sayings seem to be collected haphazardly with no obvious story line, but this raises the question of whether we might not have in *Thomas* a more faithful record of things said than we find in the canonical gospels where Jesus' teachings are rearranged into deliberately constructed "histories." Matters are not quite so simple, but at least the question leads us in the right direction by suggesting that *Thomas* is not a mere anthology of sayings drawn from Matthew, Mark, and Luke, but represents a distinct tradition all its own. Although still resisted by some New Testament exegetes, this idea has in fact come to be widely accepted today among historians of early Christianity.[7]

The *Gospel of Thomas* is not the only record of sayings about Jesus surmised to have been in circulation in the generations following his death. Luke himself cites one such saying that was not included in his gospel.[8] The most important of these collections has been referred to simply as Q (for the German *Quelle* or "source"). Its existence as a background source for the canonical gospels is generally accepted among scholars of the New Testament, even though no actual text or even reference to it has ever been discovered. And this is only one of the numerous such anthologies of sayings attributed to Jesus that the historical records of the day seem to have taken for common knowledge.

The practice of using and recording disconnected "sayings" was hardly unique to the early Christian community. It is common throughout the ancient Jewish and Greco-Roman world and can be traced back as far as the second and third millennia BCE in the ancient "Wisdom literature" of Egypt and the Middle East. Some of the wisdom is self-evident, some of it a challenge to what is taken for self-evident, but all of it is accessible as reflection on ordinary experience. We see examples of the genre in the biblical books of *Proverbs, Ecclesiastes*, the *Wisdom of Solomon*, and *Sirach*. Moreover, at the time and place that Jesus preached, the sayings of the Cynics or "dog philosophers"—the nickname given to the followers of Diogenes of Sinopes (c. 400–325 BCE) whose "useful maxims" or *chreiai* were used to shake people out of their conventional ideas and to offer an alternative way of thinking—were circulating widely.[9]

The *Gospel of Thomas* is much closer in genre to collections of such sayings than it is to the narrative form the New Testament gospels adopted to locate the words of Jesus. By the end of the first century the utility of these collections for established communities of Christians began to diminish, even as the biographical gospels continued to grow in importance. By the middle of the second century Wisdom literature itself had become something of an "anachronism."[10] And so it was that the tradition of collecting sayings came to be associated primarily with itinerant preachers and with groups of Christians who recast them in the form of dialogues between Jesus and his disciples that favored an emerging trend of Christian thought that we have come to know under the generic name of "gnosticism."[11] Leaving aside for the moment just where *Thomas* fits into this picture, it is enough to note that the blend of aphorisms, proverbs, parables, and cryptic sayings found in its dialogues is nowhere interrupted by interpretative glosses or allegorical readings of the sort we find in the canonical gospels. The words are simply left to speak for themselves, as if they had come directly from the mouth of Jesus.

THE MANUSCRIPTS

As is the case with other collections of sayings current before and after the composition of the canonical gospels, in all likelihood many of the sayings of the *Gospel of Thomas* were transmitted orally before they came to be transcribed.[12] Once in written form they continued to be passed around from hand to hand and to undergo adjustments according to the needs of those who used them and the peculiarities of the languages into which they were translated. Moreover, since these adjustments were going on at the same time as the gospels of Matthew, Mark, and Luke were taking shape, it is hard to imagine that these compositions had no effect at all on *Thomas*—or that *Thomas* had no effect on them. Aside from the ever-present possibility of simple scribal error, we have also to take into account the fact that "copying" and "translating" meant something quite different in an age where oral tradition was alive and well from one where it had died the death of distrust and succumbed to the regency of the written word. For one thing, a text used for itinerant preaching, as *Thomas* was during the time it was taking shape, would naturally be rearranged or reworded to create word-associations and keywords that would facilitate memorization.[13] For another, even with a text before them, scribes would not slavishly reproduce or translate each word or phrase. They had their own memories, their own familiarity with other texts, and some sense of what the intended audience expected of them. Today, even with the full kit of scholarly apparatus at one's disposal, separating a simple slip of the pen from a deliberate redaction is no easy matter, and it gets all the more difficult the further a text has traveled across time and space. Nothing the early Christians wrote about Jesus is exempt from this process. (For example, by the year 300 there may have been as many as five distinct versions of the Gospel of Mark being passed around in Christian communities.) Little wonder that historians shudder at attempts to elevate particular texts or parts of texts above the conditions of their birth.

In the case of the *Gospel of Thomas* the only extensive records of the process are a fragmentary set of papyri written in Greek and a complete text of the *Gospel* written in Coptic, each with its own story to tell.

The Greek manuscript is the older of the two, dating from around the end of the second century, but the text itself is considerably older, at least as old as the synoptic gospels. There is nothing particularly difficult about concluding that an earlier version existed, since the gospel is mentioned by name in written records predating the fragments that remain with us today.

When it comes to deciding just when to date it, however, there is considerable divergence among those familiar with the literary styles and languages of the century that followed the death of Jesus. The general consensus is that one or the other Greek version of the *Gospel of Thomas* was known to the authors of the canonical gospels, and that its sayings "derive from a stage of the developing sayings tradition that is more original than Q."[14] In this sense they bring us back to the earliest stages of memories about what Jesus actually said. Not that the sayings recorded were intended as an objective reproduction of Jesus' sayings, only that their selection was made at a time less removed from the historical Jesus then the canonical gospels. More precision than that, at least for now, is conjecture.[15]

Without discounting the possibility of an earlier Greek version compiled in Jerusalem by communities associated with the apostle James (known as the brother of Jesus and hence of Thomas also),[16] scholarly opinion is converging on the view that the most likely place for the composition of the Greek text that we now have was in the western Syrian city of Antioch, which Paul had used as a base for his journeys.[17] The Hellenic influence was strong there, making Greek translations both possible and necessary for revering the memory of Jesus. The Christian presence in Antioch predates Paul's arrival—in fact, it is thought to be the first place that communities referred to themselves as "Christians"—and this was to prove a source of conflict on questions of doctrine and practice. It was there that the Gospel of Matthew, to which the *Gospel of Thomas* has more parallels than to any of the other gospels, was composed.

When we consider the basic structural divergence of the two texts, and the radically distinct images of Jesus that result, we are obliged yet again to recognize that there was no such thing as Christianity but rather a plurality of Christianities separated by differences every bit as marked as their similarities. Given the varieties of language, intellectual environment, religious history, liturgical form, community organization, leadership, and theological orientation in which the sayings of Jesus were mirrored like so many colored stones tumbling around in a kaleidoscope, it is not surprising that there was so little uniformity. As obvious as this fact now looks to historians of Christianity, equally obvious is the way in which this plurality would come to be overshadowed by the uniformity imposed by a later age.[18]

All of this bears on the *Gospel of Thomas*. The written materials available today point us back to other texts and oral traditions where we simply cannot go. The fact that fragments of the Greek copy were in hand fifty years before they were identified as belonging to the *Gospel of Thomas* is some indication of just how "lost" this gospel was. In 1897 and 1903 a rubbish heap in an archaeological excavation on the site of an ancient library at Oxyrhynchus (about 160 kilometers southwest of Cairo, near a branch of the Nile at present-day Bahnasa, Egypt) turned up three papyri with sayings of Jesus that did not belong to any of the known gospels. Although the fragments were published soon after their discovery and critical reconstruction of the lacunae in them was attempted, there was no agreement on what fuller text they belonged to since they did not bear a title.[19] The transcription was dated around the year 200. The assumption at the time was that this was not the first time that Syrian and Egyptian scribes had copied— and altered—the text, but it was not until the discovery of the later Coptic translation that the hypothesis of an original Greek composition in circulation already around the latter part of the first century, prior to the authorship of the canonical gospels, could be substantiated. The Coptic translation, which has twenty sayings overlapping with the Oxyrhynchus text,[20] not only allowed that text to be clearly identified, but it also provided a touchstone for quotations and allusions to the *Gospel of Thomas* scattered throughout the writings of early historians and church fathers, which in turn provided evidence of other variants of the text since lost.

In late 1945, not far from the city of Nag Hammadi on a cliff overlooking the Nile in upper Egypt, a group of peasants happened across a sealed jar that contained the thirteen papyrus codices that have come to be known as the Nag Hammadi library.[21] The manuscripts were all written in Coptic, a late Egyptian language with a written form based on the Greek alphabet and used primarily as a means to translate texts from Greek into intelligible Egyptian.[22] Among them was a complete text of the *Gospel of Thomas*. Preserving texts in this way was a common practice up and down the Nile, but evidence suggests that this jar was *deliberately hidden*.

The origins of this Coptic translation of the *Gospel of Thomas*, whose codex is dated around 340, or a full century and a half later than the Oxyrhynchus papyri, are unknown. What is known is that although the entire Nag Hammadi collection represents translations of Greek texts spanning a period of some five hundred years, the translations into Coptic (actually two Coptic dialects) were produced in a wide area of Egypt over the course of a century and more. The extant manuscripts show the work of numerous hands.

The circumstances of the transcription of the *Gospel* and the reason for hiding it, together with other materials, are a matter of some speculation. The proximity of Nag Hammadi to Chenoboskion, the native village of Pachomius, founder of the first Christian monastery in the year 320, led to wildly different theories, from the presence of a secret sect within the monastery to the deliberate compilation of the texts as a way to become familiar with and defeat heresies. More studied scholarship suggests that both of these extremes are wrong. The care with which the copies were made suggests a reverence for the content inconsistent with the idea that they were treated as simple heresy.[23] At the same time, the monastic community appears to have been far more tolerant of the religious diversity than the rigid orthodox thinkers of the age and less hasty at drawing a line in the sand between true and false doctrine.[24] Indeed the monks seem to have been interested in currents of religious thought which both long antedated the rise of gnosticism and whose echoes can also be found in others of the Nag Hammadi texts.

This brings us to the thorniest of questions surrounding the work: the Thomas Christians and their ties to gnostic thought.

THOMAS CHRISTIANS AND
THE GNOSTIC CONNECTION

Aside from the general currency that the sayings of the *Gospel of Thomas* might have enjoyed among the early Christian communities, it has been natural to suppose that, like each of the synoptic gospels, the text would have been particularly important in defining the identity of Christians who honored the memory of the apostle Thomas in a special way, such as the Christian community in Eastern Syria did.[25] It was in this region that he was given the distinctive name of Judas Thomas, occasionally with the addition of Didymus, the Greek translation of the Aramaic nickname of "Thomas" (meaning "the twin"). The suggestion has been made, moreover, that the text was read and interpreted in a liturgical setting.[26] In recent years, however, a carefully argued case has been made that the "Thomas Christians" were not organized in established communities but were a widely dispersed group of radical itinerants, men and women,[27] with little or no structure. These wanderers would visit established Christian communities to preach their message of uncompromising homelessness and in turn would receive support from them in the form of temporary lodgings, food, and clothing. The idea is supported not only by the data that has been gathered on an early "Jesus movement" as it spread from Palestine eastwards but also by internal evidence in the text of the *Gospel of Thomas* itself.[28]

As the settled Christian communities grew more confident and came to rely more and more on the canonical gospels, the conflict with the radical element intensified, leading to the isolation of Thomas Christianity and eventually its demise. The *Gospel of Thomas* is the best proof we have of the existence of such a movement. Of itself, of course, this does not refute the possibility that established communities used the text in other ways. It seem unreasonable to suppose that they would accept the *Gospel* preached by the itinerants who happened into their midst and then set the text aside until the next visit. It is no less unlikely that the itinerants themselves used it only to preach to others, without employing it ritually among themselves or as a tool of instruction for new members. In any case, the message of *Thomas* is wider and deeper than the lifestyle of such a movement.[29]

We cannot fail to mention that the term "Thomas Christians" itself is more commonly associated with another tradition that has little or nothing to do with the *Gospel of Thomas*, namely, the belief that Thomas preached the Christian gospel in India. Allusions scattered among early church historians to the mission of Thomas identify him alternatively as the apostle to the Kingdom of the Parthians (present-day Iran) and to

India. To this day Thomas is venerated in India at the founder of Christianity there. The legend that has Jesus himself spending time in India prior to his rather late public life in Palestine and while still a member of the Essene community around the Dead Sea has been around from at least the sixth century. He is said to have traveled to India at the age of thirteen, where he lived among the Buddhists for six years. Another variant has him escaping crucifixion alive and heading east, where he met Paul, who had been dispatched to bring him back for a second crucifixion. After being nursed back to health, Jesus continued on to India, where Thomas had gone on ahead, there to spend the rest of his days until passing away in Kasmir.[30] Although the special relationship of the "Thomas Christians" with the Buddhists of south India is well known, and at least some of the literature surrounding the legend is reputable, the kernel of truth to the stories of Thomas and Jesus in India—if indeed there is one—has eluded demonstration.[31]

The cache of manuscripts among which the *Gospel of Thomas* was found provide a rich mine of information about the mysterious movement known as "gnosticism" that the early church fathers had worked so hard to expunge from Christian identity. Much of the history of gnosticism has had to be rewritten since the discovery of the Nag Hammadi library, and indeed it is still being written. For those who viewed "gnostic" tendencies as inimical to the faith, the term was synonymous with simple heresy. Not a few scholars of the Nag Hammadi library who came to feel a certain sympathy to gnostic ideas have nevertheless accepted their heterodoxy as a matter of course.[32] Not only has this been unfair to the aims of the texts, it overlooks the role that this tradition played in syncretizing Christianity into a doctrinal tradition, even if the latter would eventually exclude the former from the confines of orthodoxy.

The fact is, much first-century religious thought was gnostic, and the appearance of Jesus no doubt had an influence on it and it did not simply repudiate it. It was only in later generations that the whole of gnosticism was rendered suspect by a number of church fathers who "systematized opponents and forced them to define themselves vis-à-vis the tradition of the theologians' choice."[33] Not that there were not elements in gnosticism that could not be perceived as working against what Jesus had taught, but the Christians were not the only ones wary of certain aspects of gnosticism. The Egyptian philosopher Plotinus, for example and for quite other motives, was also critical of its excesses. Given the plurality of forms of gnosticism and a malleability that at least during its formative years it shared with early Christian thought,[34] the jostle with gnostic thought is very different from the wholesale condemnation of later-day theology.

It is therefore altogether mistaken to dismiss the gnostic tendencies of the sayings of *Thomas* as a later accretion to an originally "pure" gospel.[35] Rather, they represent a more primitive stratum of the way the sayings of Jesus were remembered and transmitted than the synoptic gospels—or even Q[36]—which introduced apocalyptic language in order to rein in those tendencies. Not only is there no clear-cut line between early Christianity and the birth of gnosticism, but, as the text will demonstrate again and again, *Thomas* itself represents a radical departure from the direction in which gnostic thought was headed.[37]

In very rough profile, gnostic ideas tended to cluster about one or the other, or both, of two central ideas: that all of creation is flawed from the start, and that there is something uncreated in the human spirit that connects us to a pristine reality prior to the world as we know it. Creation is often, though not always, viewed as the work of an errant demiurge masquerading as the transcendent God. This idea of a rebellious emanation from the true God spawned an elaborate cosmology of layers of "heavens," more or less structured according to the Middle Eastern astrology of the day. At times gnostic thought fed resentment against the idea of the Jews as a "chosen race" by identifying the culprit responsible for the created world as the Yahweh of the Old Testament. More commonly it stopped at a simple repudiation of the body and its functions as an obstacle to recognition of the truth about ourselves and our world. So overpowering was the dominion of the flesh that one could rise above it only through repeated incarnations.[38] Knowledge of the truth (*gnosis*) was thought to liberate the "unborn" light imprisoned in the darkness of matter but accessible in the inner recesses of our humanity, which is often, but again not always, viewed as an eternal, androgynous Adam.

The development of this cosmic dualism of good and evil, of spirit against flesh,[39] is absent in the *Gospel of Thomas*, where evil is seen as a function of ignorance rather than of some rebellion that occurred in the heavenly court, resulting in the creation of the world and the need for a redeemer to be sent to restore it.[40] In that sense, if *Thomas* can be called "gnostic," it is only in a drastically demythified form.[41] Nevertheless, it would come to be saddled with the entire trappings of gnostic systems altogether alien to its intentions. Irenaeus, writing around 180, does not mention the *Gospel of Thomas* by name, but it is not impossible he intended to include it in a general condemnation issued against "secret writings" about Jesus. He had little patience for collections of sayings that menaced the canon of four gospels he was interested in promoting. He writes of their compilers:

They read from unwritten sayings and, as the saying goes, undertake to weave ropes from sand; they transfer materials and reshape them and, by making one thing out of another, they lead many astray by the evilly devised fantasy of their compilations of the Lord's words.[42]

The earliest clear reference to the *Gospel of Thomas* appears around 230 in a text of Hippolytus, Bishop of Rome, who cites a passage from the *Gospel* whose wording is similar to that used by a gnostic sect known as the Naassenes.[43] Like his contemporary Origen, who condemned the text by name as apocryphal, Hippolytus rejected all but the four gospels we now recognize as canonical. By the early fourth century Eusebius of Caesarea explicitly condemned the text, claiming heretics had wrongly attributed it to the apostle Thomas. Soon thereafter Cyril of Jerusalem claimed that it had been written by wicked followers of Manicheanism, one of the two principal forms of full-blown gnosticism stemming from the early third century.[44] This string of condemnations of the *Gospel of Thomas*, inspired in large part by the attempt to organize the Christian community and to eliminate sectarian movements viewed as disruptive of the harmony of the whole, culminated in 367 with the Easter letter of Athanasius, bishop of Alexandria, demanding that the monks in Egypt who had carefully preserved the secret texts in their libraries commit everything not certified as canonical to flames. In all likelihood it was these monks, perhaps from the monastery of Pachomius, that gathered a cache of these books and hid them in a six-foot jar in the cliffs flanking the Nile where they would remain hidden for nearly sixteen centuries.

If the gnostic tinge in *Thomas* (and probably in Q as well) was all but entirely erased from the synoptic gospels in favor of a messianic theology focused on death and resurrection and better suited to the establishment of a unique Christian identity, the depiction of Peter and Matthew in *Thomas* as having failed to understand the words of the living Jesus probably indicates a complementary disregard for the ideological viewpoints *they* represent as well as for the institutional stability of the church. The author of the Gospel of John takes a more direct approach in its rejection of the *Gospel of Thomas*.[45] In organizing his account around the passion narrative, he rejects the attempts of Mark—and of the variations of Matthew and Luke—to portray Jesus as establishing a community with authoritative leadership.[46] John's Jesus addresses himself to everyone, in language that is alternately clear and enigmatic. In this latter respect, he is of one mind with *Thomas*. But there the similarity stops. The apostle Thomas (who may or may not have been the brother or even twin brother of Jesus[47]), and by obvious association anyone who subscribed to the sayings collected in the *Gospel* that bore his name, is depicted as a "doubter" who refused to *believe* what had to be *seen* (Jn 20:29).[48] The description is not inaccurate. For *Thomas* belief is not a *substitute* for wishing to see what cannot be seen but a *consequence* of seeing as much as we can of what there is to see.

The more serious problem John has with *Thomas* is a theological one.[49] In a sense it has to do with a different way of appropriating gnostic ideas into Christian thought, which opened the Gospel of John and those who accepted it to the same charges of blasphemy that it had leveled against *Thomas*. John clearly goes beyond the synoptic gospels in raising Jesus from the status of an agent of the transcendent God to an incarnate manifestation of God. For John, Jesus is the co-eternal *logos,* the word spoken from before the creation of the world, and as such is unique ("only begotten"). His Jesus claims for himself the name by which Yahweh identified himself to Moses: "before Abraham was, I am" (Jn 8:58). For *Thomas*, in contrast, Jesus is an archetype of the human person who has awakened to the divine light that we all share as having been born with the divine image impressed on our nature. Whereas the synoptic gospels stopped short of divinizing Jesus, by referring to him as the messiah (the "Christ") or a mortal endowed with supernatural powers that separate him from the rest of us, they lent themselves to a quasi-gnostic interpretation of a divine light come to illumine the earth in human form. *Thomas* takes that further step by seeing Jesus as one of us, separated only by the awareness that we are more than the everyday selves we take ourselves to be, that we are linked to God in virtue of the image of God asleep in our innermost, unknown self. In contrast, John has Thomas ask Jesus the "way," only to be told, "I am the way" (14:5), thus reasserting the uniqueness of the person of Jesus to which no one can claim the relationship of twin.

The *Gospel of Thomas* is clearly a voice outside of tradition for those who inherited the tradition after the *Gospel* was rejected as spurious. Seen from the context of its creation and use in the early centuries of Christianity, it deserves at least as much a place in the tradition as Q would, if such a thing were ever to be discovered. Archaeologically, it is better called the *first* gospel than the fifth. At least one has to wonder what Christianity would have looked like if *Thomas*, and not John, had been selected to offset the synoptic gospels.[50] But these are armchair questions. The more pressing issue is how, given the history of the Christian scriptures, we can approach *Thomas* as a sacred text.

A LENS ON THE TEXT

In spite of everything that has been said about the history and origins of the *Gospel of Thomas*, if it is to be read as a "sacred" text, knowledge of the circumstances of its birth will not suffice—and the more one is in mind of this question, the greater a hindrance it becomes. On the other hand, to approach it as a "supplement" to round out the canonical gospels ignores the unique character of the text and ultimately confounds its purpose.[51] What little historical information about Jesus and the early Christian community it does provide has the same de-inspiring effect as exegetical analysis of the text. *Thomas* is more than its origins. However dark the foot and structure of the lighthouse itself, one has to lift one's head and look at what it illumines in order to know what a lighthouse is. None of the many possibilities swirling around among scholars regarding its composition, not even the ties to gnostic thought, justifies discarding its contents out of hand, any more than what we have learned about other books of the New Testament equips us to devalue theological traditions based on erroneous information, mistranslations, or political disputes. How then do we read this text if not through the lens of received scriptural tradition? How do we read it without exiling it to the *arcana* of an underground or esoteric tradition? Must we expect *Thomas* to be loyal to the Jesus of Christian doctrine, or are we prepared to accept the possibility of infidelities as an essential part of doctrinal history itself?

The questions, although they make immediate sense, may not be the right ones to bring to the text—at least not initially. To begin with we need to encounter *Thomas* on its own terms, and that means renouncing the search for "sacred truths" that reveal to us facts otherwise beyond the reach of human understanding. In order words, to expect the *lumen revelationis* to shine through the text is to impose on it expectations foreign to the text itself. For the same reason, the questions that established theological tradition predisposes us to ask ought to be asked only *after* we have found a standpoint from which to grasp the meaning of the text. In fact, the whole purpose of the text is to lead us precisely to that standpoint. In this sense, it is not primarily a text with a particular content that can be held up for scrutiny and comparison with other contents, as it is a way of seeing. To paraphrase a celebrated phrase of Meister Eckhart, the lens through which the Christian views the text must be the lens through which the text views the Christian.[52] Unless the interpreter of *Thomas becomes* the interpreted, the text becomes no more than a dead document—a caricature of the encounter with the "sayings of the living Jesus" that is announced in its opening words.

The guiding metaphor of this encounter appears only at the end of the text, in its title: the *Gospel of the Twin*. It is not *about* the apostle Judas Thomas or even *by* him. One who has heard the words of Jesus with insight stands where Jesus stands when he speaks them. The two become like fraternal twins, distinct in outer appearance but companions from birth. The *Book of Thomas the Contender*, another of the Nag Hammadi manuscripts, whose language of disgust for the body contrasts sharply with the *Gospel of Thomas,* feigns association by aligning itself with the core idea of the latter. In the opening words Jesus (called "the Savior," a concept foreign to *Thomas*) addresses Thomas:

> "Now since it has been said that you are my twin and true companion, examine yourself and learn who you are, in what way you exist, and how you will come to be. Since you will be called my brother, it is not fitting that you be ignorant of yourself. For he who has not known himself has known nothing, but he who has known himself has at the same time already achieved knowledge about the depth of all things."[53]

As for the text of *Thomas* itself, we need not suppose that being a twin is simply a matter of private enlightenment, and for that reason fundamentally esoteric.[54] In fairness to the text, if not to its historical reputation, it is no more inherently private and esoteric than the Christian mystical tradition. *Thomas* is more likely to yield of its riches if it is approached as a form of spiritual exercise—an *ascesis*, as one of the most astute commentators on *Thomas* puts it[55]—than if it is approached as a secret doctrine, occult literature, or divination manual.[56] In other words, to understand the text by way of the new insight into ourselves it calls for, we need to open a kind of *interreligious dialogue* with the *Gospel of Thomas*.

Dialogue in its primary sense is an exercise in gleaning ideas and pulling them apart in different dialects and from different points of view; it meant arguing, discussing, and making up one's mind through words read and heard, spoken and written. Such dialogue can take place among different religious traditions only if it is recognized as a religious activity trespassing the borders that separate one tradition from another. To say that it is a religious activity does not mean that it constitutes anything like a religion itself, or that in any sense it can substitute for the symbols and history of any particular religious way. It simply means that particular religions *express* a dimension of our common humanity without *exhausting* it, and that there is always a place, a sacred place, where human individuals *of* different religious expressions can meet without each having to remain *within* the limits of their own expression. That place is the domain of no religion and yet the homeland of all religion. It is *philosophia* in its purest form, the detached, unrestricted affection for insight. It is there that we must encounter the *Gospel of Thomas* before we begin to question what, if anything, it has to offer to the Christian tradition that centuries ago rejected it.

Those who prefer their faith to be wrapped up tightly in the arms of tradition and feel no need for enhancing that faith through encounter with other religious ways or alternative readings of the tradition will, of course, shy away from the fringes of Christianity and from the locus of dialogue from which these pages are written. I have no intention of arguing against that view, but the question of just what such enhancement might mean is one we shall have to return to after our dialogue with the text.

As wide-reaching as this *Profanum* has been, there is much more to be said about the study of the *Gospel of Thomas* and its relation to other texts of the Nag Hammadi library, to late Wisdom literature, to Platonic thought, and to the variety of gnostic and hermetic ideas circulating at the time Jesus lived.[57] These are questions that involve the actual phrasing and vocabulary of the text itself. As much as this might enrich our appreciation of the text, in what follows I have decided to refrain from entering into these questions and to eliminate all references to secondary literature on the *Gospel*, to parallels with the canonical gospels, and to variants from the Coptic found in the Oxyrhynchus papyri. This is not as easy as it sounds. Because *Thomas* is set in a kind of sacred time and place, the words and phrases easily get associated with images and ideas before and after the time of the text itself. Repression of these memories is difficult in the extreme, and at times impossible to sustain.

What is more, insofar as I chose to read the text as a "dialogue," I will respect the order in which it presents itself to us, allowing its content to unfold gradually. In doing so, I have found that many of the so-called "floating logia" and "misplaced" phrases that exegetes have found are quite intelligible in their given context.

The translation of the text has been constructed in the light of the existing versions, in various languages, indicated in the concluding bibliography. The principal line-by-line commentaries I have consulted are also noted in the bibliography. Without their work, the dialogue with *Thomas* I have woven in the pages that follow would have been impossible, but to be constantly flipping the loom to show the backside of the tapestry seemed to me to diminish the clarity of the pattern that emerges when one stands face to face with the text itself.

NOTES

1. LELOUP likens the text to a string of Japanese kōan that "invites us, with paradoxical formulas, to become aware of our uncreated origin. ..." (2003, 6, 8). The architect and poet PINCHERLE, who takes rather many liberties in his translation of the text, speculates that it is closer to Hinduism or Sufism in its rejection of fasting, almsgiving, and prayer in favor of a search for one's own inner divinity (2001, 10–11); his is typical of the quest for a Jesus whose divinity the individual can share and whose message can bring us closer to Eastern religions, an old theme with growing appeal today, quite apart from the *Gospel of Thomas*. PERADEJORDI (2003) draws on Cabbalist and other parallels in his commentary.

2. A good overview of the state of the questions has been compiled by DAVIES as an Introduction to a new version of his 1980 study on the *Gospel of Thomas* (2005, 1–XLVII). See also the detailed essay of TREVIJANO (1997, 77–120). It was only after I had published these lectures that I came to know a recent study by April DeCONICK (2006), which brings together many of the loose strands in current scholarship on the *Gospel* and attempts to weave a complete and methodologically critical picture.

3. It is worth noting here that the lost (and therefore still hypothetical) collections of sayings known as Q was "in substance simply bypassed" in the composition of the Apostolic Creed (see ROBINSON 1998, 62) but were known to the authors of the synoptic gospels and freely drawn upon in their accounts of the teachings of Jesus. In fact, both the Apostles Creed and the Nicene Creed omit *all* reference to his teachings in their statement of the core of Christianity.

4. DAVIES notes that as a Galilean, Jesus' attitudes toward Judean religion would be very different from that of a Jew from Judea, thus challenging the standard image of Jesus as a rabbi who taught the Torah (2005, XXXIV).

5. As RUYSBEEK and MESSING put it, the human individual is not portrayed in the *Gospel of Thomas* as a sinner but as *unwissend* (1993, 14).

6. For a quick list of scriptural parallels see GUILLAUMONT et al. 1959, 59–62. For a more detailed exposition of similarities of contents and of the sequences of

sayings, see PATTERSON 1993, 17–110. I do not know of any scholar who would support the wild statement that it "contains the most original, purest words that we possess of Jesus the Christ." Christoph Greiner, *Das Thomas Evangelium* (Oberstaufen: Genius Verlag, 1998), 111. In contrast, the team of scholars composing the Jesus Seminar have prepared a new translation of the four canonical gospels and the *Gospel of Thomas* showing their mutual parallels and common reliance on Q, and appraising the likelihood that particular sayings represent the actual words of Jesus (FUNK et al. 1997). That said, their commentary on text, perhaps because worked out in collaboration, is remarkably thin. It is also a little disappointing to see silly remarks and anachronisms thrown into the commentary near the end of the text (525, 526, 531, 532).

7. Perhaps the most comprehensive argument for the autonomy (though not complete independence) of the *Gospel of Thomas* from the synoptic gospels has been given by PATTERSON 1993. His book is tidily summarized, with a little new material, in a short essay contained in PATTERSON et al. 1998, 33–75. The opposite view, that *Thomas* is an extraction from the synoptic gospels, has been argued and held consistently by Jacques-É. Ménard. See his *L'Évangile selon Thomas* (Leiden: Brill, 1975). John P. Meier in *A Marginal Jew: Rethinking the Historical Jesus* (New York: Doubleday, 1991, 1994) argues that material original to Matthew and taken over by Thomas proves conclusively the dependence of the latter on the former. This is consistent with his overall characterization of the entire Nag Hammadi library as pure gnosticism and lacking in historical value for our understanding of Jesus or the early Christians (1: 146–60, II: 404–5, III: 216, 562, 585). See the sharp but balanced criticisms of DAVIES (2005, XX–XXVI, XXVIII). Dominic Crossan in *The Historical Jesus: The Life of a Mediterranean Jewish Peasant* (San Francisco: Harper-Collins, 1991) takes a more sympathetic and objective approach, giving the sayings in *Thomas* the right to an equal hearing with those of the synoptic gospels. See also PATTERSON, who also takes the more reasonable approach of arguing that as *Thomas* was copied and recopied, attempts were made to "harmonize" its sayings with those of later material found in the synoptic gospels (1993, 92–3).

8. "It is more blessed to give than to receive" (Acts 20: 35).

9. Briefly documented in MEYER 1992, 16–17. On the comparison to the *chreiai* of the Cynics, see especially CROSSAN, *The Historical Jesus*, 421–2. The tradition of the Cynics lasted until the sixth century, though their sayings were used through the Middle Ages by scholars of grammar and rhetoric. In Q, Wisdom, personified as a female, speaks interchangeably with Jesus (MEYER 1992, 9).

10. DAVIES, 2005, 13. The genre of Wisdom discourse did, however, survive at least until the middle of the fourth century, as witnessed by the sayings of the Desert Masters (see the reference in VALANTASIS 1999, 15).

11. See PATTERSON 1993, 116–17, where the important scholarly contributions on the question are cited.

12. One of the richest sources of information about the oral tradition surrounding the life and teachings of Jesus, though now lost and probably of dubious reliability in any case, has been attributed to the early-second-century Phrygian bishop Papias. Mention of it is made by the fourth-century historian Eusebius. Papias seems to have been familiar

with much of the gospel material but collected oral tradition avidly. He gathered it from visitors and former disciples. Eusebius found most of it unpalatable, because Papias took things too uncritically. In any event the oral tradition itself would have been fairly muddled by that time (see GRANT and FRIEDMAN 1960, 25–8; MARKSCHIES 2002, 51–64).

13. Early on in the study of *Thomas*, G. Garitte claimed that nearly half the sayings are related to others in sequence by verbal association. "Le premier volume de l'édition photographique des manuscrits gnostiques coptes et l'Évangile de Thomas," *Le Muséon* LXX (1957): 59–73. More recently PATTERSON has tried to identify the "catchwords" that help determine the ordering of the sayings (1993, 100–2).

14. This is the studied conclusion of KOESTER in his "Introduction" to the *Gospel of Thomas*, in B. Layton, *Nag Hammadi Codex II* (Leiden: Brill, 1989), 43. It is based in part on the judgment that the sorts of apocalyptic interpretation of the Kingdom found in Q are later. It also means that when we find coincidences between *Thomas* and the sayings source Q that Matthew and Luke used to write their alternative versions of the *Gospel* of Mark, the influence of *Thomas* was indirect. FRID and SVARTVIK also take this view (2004, 42). MEYER's conclusion seems more and more representative: "An excellent case can be made for the position that the *Gospel of Thomas* is not fundamentally dependent upon the New Testament gospels, but that it preserves sayings that at times appear to be more original than the New Testament parallels" (1992, 13). PATTERSON likewise concludes that *Thomas* was "originally written more or less contemporaneous with the canonical gospel texts" (1998, 65–6).

15. For a tidy chronological outline of the composition of the gospels and their interdependence, taking into account the full range of manuscripts now in hand, see CROSSAN 1991, 427–34.

16. It is worth noting that like the *Gospel of Thomas*, the Epistle of James, although not composed by James, appeals to him as an authority. Leaving aside questions of composition, it stands out among the books of the New Testament for its proximity to the sayings tradition. See PATTERSON 1993, 178–88, and TREVIJANO 1997, 285–320.

17. FRID and SVARTVIK conclude that the oldest version of the *Gospel of Thomas* stems from the first century and circulated for some time in the Middle East and Syria before being transcribed in Greek (2004, 42). While opinion is divided on the place of origin of the original Coptic text, evidence is mounting against the view that it was produced in Eastern Syria. For a fuller, documented account of the controversy, see Michael DESJARDINS, "Where Was the *Gospel of Thomas* Written?" *Toronto Journal of Theology* 8 (1992): 121–33. The idea of a Semitic prototype, perhaps in Syrian, lying behind the Greek and Coptic versions (for example, DE SANTOS 1999, 680–1) does not have much scholarly support.

18. Elaine PAGELS has made this the subject of a recent and eminently readable little book, *Beyond Belief* (2003).

19. To be fair, Hugh G. Evelyn-White had foreseen much earlier in *The Sayings of Jesus from Oxyrhynchus* (Cambridge: Cambridge University Press, 1920) that the *Gospel of Thomas* could be the source of the fragments, but this was not accepted until after the discovery of the Nag Hammadi library in 1945.

20. The sayings in question are 1–7, 24, 26–33, 36–39, and the last half of 77. The three Oxyrhynchus fragments themselves, although clearly pointing to a more original text than the Coptic version, are from three different copies of the text.

21. A brief account of the discovery, as told by one of their number, can be found in ROBINSON 1990, 22–5, and a fuller and most enlightening retelling in Robinson's contribution to PATTERSON et al. 1998, 77–110.

22. The idea that Coptic was known to only a small, gnostic elite is still repeated (for example, PINCHERLE 2001, 10). In fact, the ties to early Christian missionaries to the dissemination of the language and its written form are too many to give much credence to the idea.

23. ROBINSON 1990, 17.

24. For a careful study of the question, see Philip ROUSSEAU, *Pachomius: The Making of a Community in Fourth-Century Egypt* (Berkeley: University of California Press, 1985), 20–8.

25. This has led some to argue that the originally Greek text may have been composed in Edessa (present-day Urfa in Turkey). See, for example, Helmut KOESTER, "Introduction," 40. On more recent theories, see note 17 above.

26. See Karen KING, "Kingdom in the Gospel of Thomas," *Foundation and Facets Forum* 3/1 (1987): 48–97. A still bolder hypothesis, first raised by Jonathan Z. Smith, is that the entire *Gospel* belongs to a baptismal rite. Although this view has the support of Steven DAVIES (2005, 136), one of the most respected scholars in the field, it seems entirely too narrow a framework for the content of the text itself. Naturally, if one believes that the *Gospel* was originally compiled "in an esoteric gnostic circle" and was esotericized to allow access by only the initiated, then the whole discussion of a Thomas Christianity is precluded from the start. For example, the commentary of PIÑERO (1999, II: 55–78) follows this line, showing an evident disdain for everything that disagrees with the canonical gospels and deliberately reading the text as if it were a generic form of gnosticism so that any gnostic similarity confirms it. In this regard he seems to rely overly on the early work of H.-C. Puech, "Doctrines ésotériques et thèmes gnostiques dans l'Évangile selon Thomas," *Annuaire du Collège de France* 62 (1962–1963): 195–203. See also DE SANTOS 1999, 681–2. The Japanese scholar ARAI Sosogu (1994, 120, 290) takes the same viewpoint, but without even attempting to take into account the wealth of research available at the time he was writing. In general his opinions rely on very early work on *Thomas* and add very little of importance to the discussion. Alas, because the rich and very different spiritual background of Japan could have helped enlighten his Western colleagues on more than one question. I include his work in the concluding bibliography because, in spite of his missing some of the most obvious nuances of the text, he occasionally touches on something of interest in his line-by-line commentary. I would also mention in this same connection the conclusion of Ramón TREVIJANO who, after a rather thorough review of the scholarly opinions on the question, tends to see everything in discord with doctrinal tradition as gnostic interference in the text (1977). Despite his many years of devotion to *Thomas* and its textual parallels to other works in the Nag

Hammadi collection, his meticulous and exemplary scholarship has not received the attention it deserves.

27. The *Gospel of Thomas* insists on the right of women to be disciples, but the problems women would face in homelessness would be greater than those of men, which makes one wonder to what extent they partook in homelessness. PATTERSON gets around the problem by suggesting that they may have disguised themselves as men to travel unmolested (1993, 155)!

28. This is the central thesis of PATTERSON, where the inspiration comes from Gerd Theissen's idea of the "wandering radicalism" characterizing the lifestyle of persons who first collected and transmitted the sayings of Jesus (1993, 131–2, 156–7).

29. Failure to see this has taken PATTERSON's otherwise attractive thesis to the unnecessary extreme of reading the whole of *Thomas* as referring to the itinerant lifestyle, a manifestation of being a chosen few standing against the majority of Christians, and their gnosticizing idea of possessing true, esoteric knowledge that sets them apart from the herd in conformity with their actual role in the Christian communities (1993, chapter 8).

30. Much of this material has been gathered together and synchronized in a rather quaint volume called *The Fifth Gospel*, by Fida HASSNAIN and Dahan LEVI (Srinagar, Kasmir: Dastgir Publications, 1988).

31. A concentrated overview of these legends and their sources can be found in RUYSBEEK and MESSING 1993, 55–70.

32. This was evident in Elaine PAGELS's *The Gnostic Gospels* (New York: Random House, 1989), but nuanced more carefully in her recent book (PAGELS 2004).

33. Rousseau, *Pachomius*, 21.

34. See Markschies 2002, 29–50.

35. A variation on this theme argues that *Thomas* was based on authentic sayings but that these were distorted and "gnosticized" by the heretical circles in which they circulated (GÄRTNER 1961, 52). This is also the guiding principle of Trevijano's studies on *Thomas* (1997, 119). See also DAVIES 2005, 26–8. On the other hand, DAVIES's conclusion that "Thomas' sophiological Christology existed prior to or in ignorance of what many call gnosticism" (147) seems to go too far in the opposite direction.

36. Scholars have come to argue for two stages, Q^1 and Q^2, to account for the shift away from wisdom sayings of Jesus toward an apocalyptic message preached by the Baptist. See KLOPPENBORG et al. 1990, 171–245.

37. This is the conclusion of the patriarchs of the Nag Hammadi research, Helmut Koester and James Robinson, cited in PATTERSON 1993, 106–9. In addition, KOESTER has noted that whatever there is of gnosticism in Thomas, "It is not possible to ascribe the work to any particular gnostic school or sect." See his introduction to "The Gospel of Thomas (II, 2)," in ROBINSON 1990, 125–6.

38. GÄRTNER, who is already predisposed to reading *Thomas* as a gnostic testament, bends over backward to find evidence of this in saying 109 of the *Gospel* (1961, 137).

39. In an essay originally published in 1994 I took issue with scholars who read a gnostic depreciation of the body into Thomas, arguing that, on the contrary, the idea of

illumination that it advances shares with Buddhism the demand for a restoration of the senses to their full capacity. Reprinted in Spanish as "Recuperar los sentidos: Contra una época de asceticismos," *Diálogos a una pulgada del suelo: Recuperar las creencias en una época interreligiosa* (Barcelona: Editorial Herder, 2005), 95–136.

40. I find it odd that someone as familiar with the text and as skeptical of identifying it as a gnostic text as Stephen Patterson should not only find gnostic dualism in *Thomas* but a presentation of Jesus as a "redeemer come from God into a hostile and evil world to rescue a stranded race of chosen ones" (PATTERSON et al. 1998, 53, 59–61).

41. This deliberate distancing from fundamental gnostic mythology makes it hard to accept the conclusion of Pearson ("De nyfunna gnostiska handskrifterna från Nag Hammadi," *Svensk religionshistorisk årsskrift* 1: 64–73) that "the Coptic GT is a gnostic redaction of a non-gnostic gospel." CIVRA tends in the same direction to assume too heavy a gnostic influence on the theology of *Thomas*, which he sees as a palliative to the "enthusiastic but stubborn-headed" Paul (2001, 17) and to see the purpose of the text as "underlying and reinforcing" gnostic thought (67).

42. *Adversus haereses*, 1.8.1.7. These and further references can be found in GRANT and FREEDMAN 1960, who were the first to carefully track down allusions to the text in the church fathers. Still, their work is flawed by a rather surprising agreement with the criticism they found there, arguing that Thomas represents "a warping of the lines laid down in our gospels," and that because it lacks a historical account it is "essentially gnostic, not Christian" (108). Part of the problem is that they did their work before the rest of the Nag Hammadi library had been published, assuming that its gnostic character text would be reconfirmed by the rest of the manuscripts (105). What happened was the opposite, and their contortions to interpret everything as gnostic read rather ridiculously to us today.

43. The passage reads: "He who seeks me will find me in children over seven years old; for there, in the fourteenth age, though hidden I shall be manifest" (*Ref.*, 5.7.20). The passage echoes sayings 3–5 of Thomas. Ironically, Hippolytus himself broke from the church of Rome over a doctrinal dispute and set himself up as antipope, only to be reconciled again at his death.

44. In the late fifth century Gelasius, the first pope to condemn the text by including it in a kind of "Index of forbidden works," also saw it as Manichean.

45. Many of the scholarly conclusions from research on the relationship between the gospels of Thomas and John can be found in PAGELS 2004, 45–91, in fact the only section that has to do with the subtitle of her book, "The Secret Gospel of Thomas."

46. It is significant that at the time John's gospel was composed, Ignatius of Antioch was writing his letters (100–18), promoting the hierarchical organization of the church in imitation of Jesus and disciples, the idea of martyrdom as a way of imitating Christ, and a sacramentally based community centered on the Eucharist. John avoided any association with hierarchy or a sacramental system. "The ideal type for John is the beloved disciple; the ideal type for Ignatius is the monarchial bishop" (VALANTASIS 1999, 19).

47. Meier rejects out of hand the idea, advanced by Koester and others, on the basis of a traditional belief among Syrian Christians, that Judas Thomas and Jesus were broth-

ers (*A Marginal Jew,* III: 256). Aside from the obscure reference in Mark 6:3 to Judas as one of the "brothers of Jesus" (the others being Joseph, James, and Simon, not to mention his sisters), the Syrian *Acts of Thomas* has Jesus declare, "I am not Judas who is also called Thomas, but his brother" (cited in PATTERSON et al., 1998, 38). TREVIJANO dismisses the idea of Koester and others that Thomas was a brother of Jesus as "a later confusion rather than an early tradition" and therefore rightly "repressed by orthodoxy" (1997, 310, 83).

48. DeCONICK (2001) insists that even if John did not know the *Gospel of Thomas* or the community of Thomas Christians, there is no denying that he is "polemicizing against it." Gregory Riley not only accepts that John was in contact with the "rival community" of Thomas but states explicitly what I have mentioned in the text: that John actually invented the figure of Doubting Thomas to hold up the beliefs of the Thomas Christians to ridicule. See his *Resurrection Reconsidered: Thomas and John in Controversy* (Philadelphia: Fortress, 1995), 122–3. Note that John earlier refers to him by the odd name of "Thomas, the one called Didymos" (11:16). (See also FRID and SVARTVIK, 2004, 46.)

49. On the investigation of overlaps of terms and concepts with John, see DAVIES (2005, 106–16).

50. The suggestion is PAGELS'S (2004, 54).

51. This seems to me the fundamental failure of KOCH 2003, who absorbs the *Gospel* into the biography of Jesus *ad libitum* without sufficient respect for what is known about the history of the text. A similar attempt to reconcile *Thomas* with the traditional image of Jesus, though in the form of a commentary, can be found in WINTERHALTER (1988).

52. This is how I understand the insistence of VALANTASIS (1999, 7) that the theology of *Thomas* is primarily a *performative* theology that is incomplete without the creation of a "new and alternative subjectivity" (12) in the reader.

53. ROBINSON 1990, 201. I adjusted the final phrase to read "all things" in place of "all," in line with objections that the latter sounds like a technical, neoplatonic term, which in this context it is not. Both PAGELS (2003, 57) and WINTERHALTER (1988, 12–13) cite this passage in support of the reading of *Thomas* as an initiation to become ourselves Jesus' "twins." WINTERHALTER'S excessive reference to parallels in the *Odes of Solomon*, which is clearly of later origin than *Thomas*, runs the risk of reading back into the text interpretations that are not there. There are numerous other problems with his trust in word-association for finding parallels to the New Testament, including John, that make it difficult to read the commentary without considerable caution.

54. This is KOESTER'S conclusion, reached on the grounds that the *Gospel* offers "divine Wisdom as the truth about the human self" ("Introduction," 49–50). Others who bring a neo-gnostic bias to the text, although often perceptive in their reading, lean in the same direction. Thus: "It is no longer a question of 'commenting' on the words of Jesus but of 'meditating' on them in the soil tilled by our silence. We believe that just there, more than in mental agitation, it can bring its fruit to light..." (LELOUP 2003, 10). "The only essential thing is self-awareness, the inner search; this is the only thing to seek

to do the will of the Father and enter in his Kingdom that is already here, hidden, within the ego" (PINCHERLE 2001, 15).

55. The purpose of the *ascesis* is not to repress worldly desires but to form new habits. As such it is something that cannot be accomplished vicariously or as a group, but its consequences extend beyond the individual (VALANTASIS 1999, 21–4).

56. Frankly I find the suggestion of DAVIES (2005, 149–69) that the *Gospel of Thomas* was used as a divination manual ridiculous, both because of its impracticality as a text and because of the absence of proof that such a culture existed among the early Christians.

57. I would mention here FRID and SVARTVIK (2004) and MEYER (1992), both of which provide a rich and astounding selection of parallels to gnostic and patristic literature, as well as to biblical parallels. But even this is only a small fraction of the web of textual relationships onto which *Thomas* opens.

Fanum

Dialoguing with the text

As CHILDREN of our times, we need to take care not to be detained so long in the *profanum* of the *Gospel of Thomas* that the sacredness of the text becomes subservient to the balance of scholarly opinion. To enter the *fanum* is to enter a different world. Not to recognize this is to risk the profanity of inoculating ourselves against being inspired by what we find there.

Given all the perils and complexities that went into the production of a scripture like *Thomas*, to call it "sacred" requires that one broaden the notion of the sacred beyond the actual printed words to include the continual process of selection that went into its creation. And if one is to sacrilize that process, then there is no reason to assume that the selection involved in reading, interpreting, and transmitting the text in our own times should qualify as simple profanation. In the *profanum*, we sought synchronicity with the text itself. In the sacred precincts of the *fanum* we seek synchronicity with the voice that speaks in it, to stand where Jesus stands, to inherit a wisdom for our own time and circumstances.

These are the secret words that the living Jesus spoke and Didymos Judas Thomas wrote down.

Here we have the original description or "incipit" of the text, whose identification as a set of secret sayings seems to instruct the reader that what follows belongs to the genre of other such collections in circulation. As we will see, however, the secrecy of the sayings in *Thomas* is of another sort. It is not a function of some esoteric gnosis reserved for those initiated into a clandestine inner circle, or of some hidden meaning that is the special privilege of an elite few who possess the code to deciphering the sayings. On the contrary, since most of the sayings were already widely known and many of them would find their way later into other gospels, the reason for their secrecy must lay elsewhere. At the same time, since it is the words that are said to be secret (*apokrypha*) and not their *meaning*, we have to ask just what it is that keeps them from being open and available to all. Until we know more, we can only resign ourselves to the expectation that we are about to be exposed to something out of the ordinary.

The attribution of the sayings to a living Jesus might be thought to refer to words spoken by one resurrected from the dead, or perhaps by a docetic or "semblance" Jesus who is believed to live in an eternal realm and never to have been born or died on earth at all. For now, it is best to reserve judgment and wait for the meaning of this unusual title to be revealed. Unlike the familiar titles the canonical gospels reserved for Jesus—Son of Man, Son of God, Savior, Redeemer, Christ, Messiah—this one is unconventional enough to make us wonder if the image of Jesus we are about to meet is so different that none of these titles fit.

The name of the transcriber of the sayings, Didymos Judas Thomas, only heightens the suspense. The historical person, Judas "the twin" (Thomas in Aramaic, Didymos in Greek), is known to us as one of the immediate disciples of Jesus, and there is nothing surprising about seeing his name associated with a *florilegium* of the sayings of his master. But the fact that he was reputed to be the brother—even the twin brother—of his own spiritual master, suggests that what we are about to read will give us a very different insight into what Jesus had to say from what those who came to know Jesus in his adult life have had to say.

---

1. And he said, "Whoever finds the meaning of these words will not taste death."

We are not told who speaks the opening lines of the *Gospel*, but the most obvious choice is Thomas. This means that the text either wants us to suppose that Thomas, who we were just told is the "writer," is writing about himself in the third person, or that someone else is telling the story based on transcriptions made by Thomas. If we substitute the nickname of the "author," we have "And Jesus' Twin said," and yet another possibility opens up: The one who is telling us about what was said is not a historical person at all but a narrator created for a purpose other than the production of an accurate record of things heard. This would make sense if we assume, as we must in the case of a text whose contents were passed from mouth to mouth and that went through so many revisions, the work was a group effort. The purpose of the narration would then be to draw the reader into the sayings themselves and divert attention from any purely objective meaning they might have in themselves. In other words, without the engagement of the reader, the text is incomplete, the words of a *dead* Jesus. As for Judas Thomas the annotator, his role would be that of a *legitimizing fiction* to give unity to the whole and to give it authority as a gospel. This is reinforced by the fact that the proper name of Judas is omitted from the title of the *Gospel* that appears at the end of the text: *The Gospel of Thomas*. In addition, from this point onward the historical person of Judas Thomas disappears from the text, and in his place we have simply Thomas, "the twin." Just who—or what—this twin represents, and what relationship he has to the living Jesus are questions we must hold in suspense for now. Once we have grasped that relationship, there will be no difficulty understanding the sense in which he refers to Jesus and to Thomas.

What the Twin has to tell us is spoken from the standpoint of one who already has found the meaning of these words, one for whom the secret has come to light. If we can stand where the Twin stands, we will know what it means not to taste death. It is not Jesus in the first place who holds out that promise, as we might expect, but Jesus' Twin, who seems to speak from somewhere deep behind the words that death cannot touch. It is not said that we will escape the fate of all human beings to die, or that we will somehow resurrect on the other side of death. We are simply left with the hint that whatever there is to be tasted here is different from other things of life that satisfy us for a moment only to leave us finally with a sense of dissatisfaction. In this first saying we have the touchstone for everything that follows: The only guarantee that we have understood what the Twin has understood is that it does not leave the taste of death in our mouths.

---

2. *Jesus said, "Let those who seek not stop seeking until they find. When one finds, one will be troubled. When one is troubled, one will marvel and rule over all."*

As we saw already in logion 1, the narrator records the sayings, themselves spoken in the present, in the past tense. "Jesus says" would invite us to enter a world beyond time, to encounter a Jesus who speaks directly to us in a kind of eternal now. It would be no more than a literary device to separate one time-

less truth from the next. This is clearly not the purpose of this
Gospel. The voices we hear are voices from the past telling us
something that we need to understand in the present. Those
who said the words have died and left us; but there is something in the words that has not died. Objectively speaking,
Jesus probably said very few of the things attributed to him
here, and those who selected, compiled, and edited the sayings were no doubt aware of it. The use of the past tense is not
intended to simulate the recording of historical facts. It lends
authority to the sayings, not the authority of the person who
spoke it but the authority of one who knows what he is talking
about from experience. By the same token, by sharing in that
experience we can stand where the speaker stood and make his
voice our own.

In other words, our task is to search for ourselves what the
speaker has already found but which cannot be communicated
simply in words. Without that search, the sayings belong irre-
trievably to the unrecoverable past. Yet the search is a peculiar
one, different from the usual meaning of looking for something until we find it. For one thing, we expect to be told just
what it is we are supposed to be looking for, but we are not. At
most we can assume that it has something to do with the interpretation of these words. For another, the only assurance we
are given of knowing that we have found what we were looking
for is that we will be more troubled than when we started. This
is a marvel that awaits us, to transform us from persons controlled by our search to persons reigning over all things.

If this sounds terribly abstruse, it is because the goal is not
to set us out on some mysterious quest but to address the bias
we bring to the process of searching and finding: *I*, a subject,
set out to find some *thing*, the object of my search. I am either
satisfied when I have the object in hand or frustrated when I

do not. It matters not if that something is a physical object, a person, or a state of mind; the process remains the same. In a sense, by knowing what it is one is seeking, one has already found it in part; otherwise we would not recognize it when we found it. Not in this *Gospel*. Here completion of the search is not the result of changing from a seeker to a finder, while the object of the search remains the same. It ends in the realization that when it comes to reigning over all things, the pattern of seeking-and-finding is an illusion. It is never said that we will find what it is we are seeking. On the contrary, the intimation is that *finding entails a transformation of seeking, not putting an end to it.* This intimation will be borne out later when we have a clearer idea what this reign entails. A first indication appears in the following logion.

3. *Jesus said, "If your leaders say to you, 'Look, the kingdom is in heaven,' then the birds will get there before you. If they say to you, 'It is in the sea,' then the fish will get there before you. Rather, the kingdom is within you and outside you. When you know yourselves, then you will be known, and you will understand that you are children of the living father. But if you do not know yourselves, then you are in poverty and you are poverty."*

As familiar as the phrase the kingdom is within you sounds, it already has a different meaning in this *Gospel*, and that because "you" means "we" who are now part of this text. The words are not addressed to a generic audience but directly to the reader, the one who we just heard needs to learn all over again what it means to seek for the things that really matter. The *Gospel* does not speak of a Kingdom of God or a Kingdom of Heaven, which suggests some future eschaton or at least a world beyond whose arrival we can only prepare for and acquiesce to when it comes. It does not imagine, as we might from comparing it to the kingdoms of the world, a heavenly court ruled by a single divine Monarch to which we belong as subjects. It is rather a kingdom in which each individual is king, in which it is within the power of each and every one to rule over all things.

At the same time, the logion does not tell us that the kingdom is only within the human person. To do so would only be to invite a new dualism, between the outer world and an inner kingdom, to replace the one it is rejecting. Far from depreciating the wider world in which we live, it speaks of a kingdom that is both within us *and* without us—a kingdom *whose center is everywhere and whose circumference is nowhere.* The surest way to obscure that kingdom from view is to seek it as something far away, deep in the sea or high in the skies. The words of Jesus are meant to direct our search away from what lies above and away to a point at which everything—including the sea and the sky—to be found is near at hand. To stand there, at that point, is to know oneself and to be known.

It is not yet clear just what knowing that one is known has to do with the kingdom, but let us take the text as it stands and not assume a *lapsus calami* for "you will know the kingdom." Rather than fault the *Gospel* for obscurity of expression, we need to see such dropping of hints before they can make sense as ways of insinuating the reader more deeply into the text. All that we are told here, in sharp, almost sarcastic language, is that the opposite of a kingdom in which one rules over all things is a state of bondage that those who guide you would have you believe is the real kingdom, and that height of such bondage consists in not even knowing that one is being dominated. This is what the *Gospel* calls the poverty of not knowing who you are. It is not just that one lives in the poverty of this darkness of ignorance; one *is* that poverty. Only a conversion of the idea of who I think I *am* can bring me to the wealth of ruling over all things as children of the living father.

As much as we might like to identify the living father with a transcendent, creator God, the text does not require this of us. Nor does it tell us what it is that makes Jesus, and now the father, living. It only says that insight into who we are will tell us something about our true parentage and help us understand what it means to think of ourselves, and to be thought of, as children again. The next logion begins at that point.

4. Jesus said, "The person old in his days will not hesitate to ask an infant of seven days about the place of life, and that person will live. For many who are first will be last, and will become a single one."

It was a matter of common knowledge for Jesus and his followers that the first contact an infant would have with "those who guide" is on the eighth day after birth, when it is presented in the temple for the rite of circumcision and given the name by which it will be known in society. And is common sense that it is the prerogative of elders to instruct the young about the things that matter most in life. It is not without deep irony, then, this logion should draw a scene in which an old man consults a child, who has not yet been initiated into the place of religion, about the place of life, and in so doing is led to live in a way he had not lived before. The first thing we are told about this place of life, then, is that it is *not* in the precincts of religious convention and common sense, but somewhere closer to the point of origin from which these have distanced us, a place where those whom we consider the first often end up the last.

Well and good, but what has a child of seven days to teach an old man? It cannot even *speak* let alone answer questions about life. What it has to communicate is done without words. Who of us has not stood over an infant and admired the brightness in its eyes as it tries to take in its surroundings, or the unquestioning sensuality of its contact with everyone and everything about it, and not felt at some moment the desire to return to that point where the relationship between the senses and the world is unimpeded by habit. If the mind of the infant represents a pure sensuality that has not yet been compromised—or enhanced—by language and ideas, and if this has something to do with seeking the kingdom, then one of the marks of having found it must lie in a *restoration of the senses*. If finding the place of life has something to do with rejuvenation, this is as young at heart as one already experienced in the things of life can hope to get.

There is no need to read the words about the inverting of the order of who comes first and who comes last as simply a cynical reproach against the customary categories by which we measure one another. There is a more positive sense, which is captured in the idea of becoming one. When we say of an old man who has recovered something of the spark of youth has achieved a "new unity" in his person, this does not imply that he was fragmented before that but only that one unity gives way to another. So, too, when we speak of the first and the last changing places, this does not make them one and the same. It means only that there is a standpoint from which their distinction is irrelevant.

To understand the importance of the final sentence of this logion for the *Gospel* we have to see it as a commentary on the preceding examples. That is, we need to take a step back and have a deeper look at the conversion that they call for in our way of thinking. To understand how knowledge of the place of life passes over the distinction between old and young, first and last it is necessary to understand the sense in which such categories are an obstacle to that knowledge. The best way to expose our habit of thinking in those terms is to see what kind of judgments would result if we rid ourselves of it. The two examples in this logion accomplish just that by reversing the usual order of things. By placing the accent on a conversion away from thinking in dichotomies, that is to say, on becoming one, the idea of ruling over all things is purified of any sense of simply reversing roles—the child with the elder, the last with the first, the subject with the king. Instead it holds out the possibility of finding a place of life where those distinctions cease to matter. At the same time, the fact that children are much closer to that place, and the infant of seven days even more so in virtue of an unconditioned oneness with the world around it that will shatter as it develops a social identity, suggests a special relationship between the immediacy of experience of the child and the goal of ruling over all things. Of this the *Gospel* will have more to say later.

> 5. *Jesus said, "Know what is in front of your face, and what is hidden from you will be disclosed to you. For there is nothing hidden that will not be manifest."*

The reference to secret sayings in the incipit is here clarified to remove any doubt about their containing occult or arcane ideas. We are told, in unambiguous language, that what is hidden is a result of our not *seeing* what is staring us in the face, and that this is true of *everything* that is hidden. Read in tandem with the previous logia, we are being told that the self-knowledge that will allow us to rule over all things is no further away from us than we are from ourselves. Still, we are not given any indication of how this manifestation will take place or what our role is to be. Indeed the impression we are left with thus far is that our only task is to stop looking in the wrong places for that which really matters. In that sense, it is not only the kingdom that will become manifest but the biases in our thinking that occlude it from sight. The nature of the relationship between seeking and finding is slowly coming into focus: If you cannot see what is right in front of you, what you are looking for will not find you.

When the *Gospel* recycles well-known phrases, like the latter half of this logion, it is not to reiterate their conventional meaning. It wrenches them from their original context and associations and relocates them, obliging the reader to do the work of uncovering their meaning. In this case, the new meaning includes, in addition to what was just indicated, a reference to the *Gospel* as a whole. It is not only the darkness surrounding about the kingdom that will be lifted when one comes to know the truth about oneself, but the secrecy covering these sayings will be unveiled: There is nothing *apocryphal* that will not become *revelation*.

> *6. His disciples asked him, "Do you want us to fast? How should we pray? Should we give alms? What dietary regulations should we observe?"*
>
> *Jesus said, "Do not lie, and do not do what you hate, because all things are revealed in the sight of heaven. For nothing is hidden that shall not be manifest, and nothing is covered that will remain undisclosed."*

This is the first time the disciples appear in the *Gospel*, informing us that Jesus' words have an immediate audience. And in fact it is their presence that allows us to read the text as a flowing discourse in which things that are unclear at one moment become clearer at another.

Jesus does not give a direct answer to the question that he is put in this logion, but summarily rejects the premises on which it is based, namely, that these are matters of primary importance and that following the dictates of traditional religious observance has intrinsic value on its own. Only after this has been clarified can the question be answered. Since prayer, fasting, and diet were the cornerstones of Jewish practice, and almsgiving revered from ancient times, the fact that all four are swept aside so quickly confirms the rejection in logion 3 of those who guide us to look for the kingdom where it is not. As the final sentence, a repetition of the previous logion, tells us, this is an example of the manifestation of something right in front of our face: a bias that impedes our vision without our being aware of it.

The counsel not to do what you hate has a double-edge to it. On the one hand, it exposes the lie of going through the motions of a ritual practice merely out of a sense of obligation. This takes us a step closer to understanding where the dualism of judging things according to accepted categories (logion 4) is rooted, namely in the duality of following conventions and disregarding what is in our hearts. On the other hand, it implies that we ought to *do only what we love to do.* But to know what one *loves,* as distinct from knowing what one *wants* at any particular moment, requires that we know ourselves for who we are. As of yet, we still have no idea of how the *Gospel* understands that term. The only intimation we are given here is that it involves seeing ourselves and all things plain in the sight of heaven. Here again, we must refrain from reading into that phrase any particular idea of an all-seeing eye monitoring us from on high. It simply means finding a point to stand under the bright blue sky where nothing is hidden from our sight, in other words, finding the standpoint from which Jesus himself is speaking.

> *7. Jesus said, "Blessed is the lion that the human will eat, so that the lion becomes human; and cursed is the human that the lion will eat, and the lion will become human."*

As strange as this image sounds to us, and as alien from anything that has gone before, we have no choice but to take it at face value rather than run off to rummage through the history of near-Eastern symbolism for an explanation. Despite all the parallels that exist in a variety of different religious traditions, the *Gospel* is using it for its own purpose. It is up to the one who has been entangled in the text to discern what that purpose must be. Given everything that has gone before, the answer is not far off.

To begin with, we recall that the previous logion asked about observing a certain diet, to which Jesus' response was to rephrase the question in order to focus on the duality of ignoring what we love by doing what we hate. The image of this logion paraphrases that answer. If there is something—or some force—of deep unhappiness within us that is capable of making us live a lie by doing what we hate, of keeping us from knowing who we are, it is not destructive because of what *it* is but because *we* have not understood it. It is not some sort of evil demon that needs to be driven out of us or annihilated, but an errant part of ourselves that needs to be appropriated into self-understanding, made part of our humanity. Only when the lion is eaten and integrated into the fullness of our humanity can it be transformed from a curse into a source of happiness. In the measure that it is not understood and appropriated, the lion eats away at our humanity from within, the lower side battening and growing stronger on the higher, a curse disintegrating our humanity. We become more lion than human. (The repetition of the identical phrase "and the lion will become human," for opposite meanings is a device we shall meet with often in the *Gospel* as a way of indicating a change of mind or perspective.)

The fragmenting effect of conventional thinking and mindless religious observance that keeps me from becoming one flows out of and feeds back into the powerful drive to be guided by ways of thought and practice that I know, in my heart of hearts, I hate. Only by seeing through that impoverishing and all-consuming illusion can I come to the place of life where I can see that what I am truly seeking has already found me and stands right before my face.

> *8. And he said, "The human being is like a sensible fisherman who threw his net into the sea. He drew it up from the sea and it was full of small fish. The fisherman found among them a fine large fish. He threw all the small fish back into the sea and chose the large fish without hesitation. Whoever has ears to hear, let them hear."*

This is the first and only time the *Gospel* explicitly makes the human being the subject of a parable, and the second time that the ambivalent and still unexplained "he said" is used to describe the speaker. Earlier we suggested that it might refer to both Jesus and Thomas. We still do not know what that would mean, but at least we are reminded that the question remains unanswered.

The logion continues the description of becoming one—that is, an integrated human being—by telling us that the effort of seeking is not enough. One must be sensible and on the watch for the moment when that which matters most drops unexpectedly into our boat. When it does, the sensible thing to do is to throw the common sense of a working fisherman, and with it the rest of one's catch, into the sea without hesitation. Our curiosity about just what this large and fine fish that renders one's usual way of valuing things irrelevant might be is not satisfied. Nor is there any suggestion that we should read the story as an allegory and try to figure out what the sea, the small fish, and the net mean. Instead, a standard bit of proverbial, even playful wisdom is appended at the end as if to say, "Wait and listen."

> *9. Jesus said, "Behold, the sower went out, took a handful of seeds, and scattered them. Some fell on the road and the birds came and pecked them up. Others fell on rock; they did not sink roots into the soil and produce heads of grain. Others fell among thorns; they choked the seeds and worms ate them. And others fell on good soil and produced good fruit—sixty measures and one hundred twenty measures."*

Without stopping to explain, another parable follows on the heels of the last. Once again, the worker is a model of incompetence at his profession. The production of good fruit is entirely a matter of chance for one who throws seeds to the four winds without concern for where they land. Apparently it is not enough for good ground and seeds to come together; any experienced farmer could see to that. But here it takes a foolish sower to get spectacular results, which leaves the reader with the nagging question of whether *this* sower might know something that his fellow farmers do not. If so, then there is a more radical irony in the parable: something as ordinary as scattering seeds is used not to *apply* the innocent conventional wisdom of the farmer to some spiritual matter but to *make light of it.*

And once we have looked at the tale from that standpoint, we have to stop and think whether there is anything more noble about seed producing fruit than nourishing birds or worms. In a word, we are invited to a transformation of perspective whereby the ordinary values by which we judge the things of life are held in suspense, the better to see, just as it is and without judgment, what is right in front of our face.

> *10. Jesus said, "I have thrown fire on the world, and behold, I am watching over it until it blazes."*

This image of Jesus as one who starts a fire and watches over it is important to the *Gospel*. He does not say it is *he* who fans it, but only that he guards it. Since it is lit without distinction on the whole of the world, one is tempted to think it the spark that will ignite a great apocalyptic conflagration that will consume everything evil in the world and usher in the new order that he seems to be talking about. That would completely change the tone of the *Gospel* up to this point, and in any case is not what he actually says. We have to assume that the fire he is talking about does what fire does, and no more. It illumines by transforming; something is gained by something being lost. Given that the one who casts this fire on the earth has just been criticizing social and religious conventions, we have some idea what it destroys, but not yet of what is illumined in the process.

> *11. Jesus said, "This heaven will pass away and the heaven above it will pass away. The dead do not live and the living will not die. In the days when you ate what was dead, you made it alive. When you come into the light, what will you do? On the day when you were one, you became two. But when you have become two, what will you do?"*

In content and structure, this next logion is strange and unexpected. It is as if Jesus himself, disappointed with the straightforward questions of his disciples, puts the kind of question he expects them to be asking themselves. He begins with a series of statements indicating a total reversal of the order of things, statements intended to make them marvel and at the same time to disturb them, as if to remind them of what they were told at the outset to expect.

When the sky overhead loses its meaning as pointing to a higher, heavenly realm, and the very *idea* of such a heaven disappears; when the revered dead figures of the past no longer live on in memory and those who are now alive take their place as the immortals; when one can no longer consume the past and so breathe life into what is dead—then one will have stepped into the light. And then what is to be done?

If we read this logion as a continuation of the former, then Jesus is asking his followers to consider carefully the consequences of fanning the flickering flame he has lit into a bright torch that will make them see things in a new light. The important questions are not what particular religious practices to keep up and which to discontinue, but how to keep one's balance when the beliefs one relied on have been turned inside out.

The announcement that the values of those who have died and gone before us are passing away leaves us without a place to stand. Jesus hints that he knows something that is more alive and will not die. As we just saw, there is no suggestion of an impending end of the world as such but only of the way we see the world. One must find a way to stand in the light he has cast on the world. We watch our world disintegrate in the flames. What was once one is seen to be two. As the duality hidden within our ideas of heaven and earth, of what is alive and what is dead, comes to light, we must ask ourselves, What will we do then? How will we find a new integration, how to find that place of life where things become one again, where the kingdom can be seen as without and within?

In this attempt by Jesus to draw the disciples into the meaning of his words, the *Gospel* draws the reader in along with them. The deliberately oracular tone reminds us that what the secret sayings need to come alive is not an audience but a questioning.

The relationship between light and life in this logion recapitulates and reinforces what we have understood thus far. The light and everything that stands within it is completely exposed, leaving nothing hidden. Hence a life standing in the light would be uncontaminated by the false dichotomies that knowledge standing in the dark relies on. Quite the contrary, it would enable us to recognize the illusions of conventional thinking that have kept us in ignorance. It begins, therefore, with a kind of *unknowing* of what we thought we knew. To live in the light is to awaken as it were from a slumber where we savored what was dead thinking it alive. Those who have found the place of life do not taste death in the things of life but restore them to new life.

There is one more thing that is troubling about this saying. It is not just that the unity of *ideas* is fractured to disclose the illusory dichotomies we need in order to know and value the things of life. Our unity as persons is broken. Where we were one, we become two. We are not the merely ordinary, everyday selves we are used to thinking we are. We harbor an other. Since that revelation comes to us standing in the light, we must assume that it is not an *alius* but an *alter*. At the same time, since this duality is not illusory but belongs to life, the nature of its unity must be different from the unity that is consumed in the light of the fire. It must be something that does not burn because it is already fire. It must, in a sense we do not yet understand, be capable of integrating the opposites and not simply imply that one element conquer or absorb the other. Clearly to become one we must first become two. In this sense, the *Gospel* does not simply reject all dualism but only dualism that is static and does not lead to a new unity.

> *12. The disciples said to Jesus, "We know that you will be leaving us. Who will be our leader?"*
>
> *Jesus said to them, "Wherever you are, you are to go to James the Just; heaven and earth came into being for his sake."*

Despite the hint about what is the right question to ask, the disciples fail to grasp the point. This time, however, Jesus' reaction does not show the same impatience as before but honors them with a direct answer, or at least with what seems to be a direct answer. If they need to go somewhere, he tells them, then let it be with James. The disciples would have understood what he meant. Of all the communities that were taking shape, the one that formed in Jerusalem around James and continued to recognize his authority after he had died is recommended. There they would find the strict asceticism and observance of Jewish rituals that had earned James the nickname of the Just. The proverbial form of praise for great figures "for whose sake heaven and earth came into being," as with all such conventional religious wisdom, should not be taken to imply any literal connotation of a divine creator, of which the *Gospel* makes no mention. By telling the disciples that, from the viewpoint of their question, James is "the first among you," he is setting the stage for the reversal of rank he announced in logion 4. The place they wish to go and the desire for someone great among them is obviously not the same as the place of life to which Jesus is directing them. They have a choice, but first they have to understand what that choice entails. Jesus throws the question back at them in the next logion.

> *13. Jesus said to his disciples, "Compare me to something and tell who I am like."*
>
> *Simon Peter said to him, "You are like a righteous angel."*
> *Matthew said to him, "You are like a wise man."*
>
> *Thomas said to him, "Master, my mouth is altogether incapable of saying what you are like."*
>
> *Jesus said, "I am not your master. Because you have drunk, you are inebriated from the bubbling spring that I measured out."*
>
> *And he took him and went aside and told him three things. When Thomas returned to his companions, they asked him, "What did Jesus say to you?"*
>
> *Thomas said to them, "If I tell you one of the things he said to me, you will pick up stones and cast them at me. And fire will come out of the stones and consume you."*

In order to get behind the disciples' question concerning who should be the great one among them after he has gone, Jesus takes the ironical position of asking them to describe, on their terms, who they think he is like. Their answers confirm his suspicions that they do in fact think in terms of comparison with what they already know and hence have not understood him, even though what they say is not unreasonable and in some sense is even fitting—only not *their* sense. Jesus is not eliciting the act of faith in himself they think he is. Simon Peter's comparing him to an angel would be appropriate had he understood it to mean that he is the bearer of a good message (a gospel), but the addition of the qualification just reiterates what he understood as Jesus' affirmation of James the Just in the former saying: a herald of orthodox belief and practice. Matthew's choice of the title of philosopher would be acceptable had he understood it in the sense of a lover of wisdom, but the qualification "wise" puts Jesus on a pedestal he has no intention of occupying.

Only Thomas gives the answer Jesus is looking for, and even if not completely so. The title Master is immediately rejected as inconsistent with the rest of what Thomas says, or rather refuses to say because he cannot find the words. At the same time, Thomas is cautioned against becoming intoxicated with his insight, lest it dull his senses and delude him into thinking he alone has been chosen for a secret knowledge. When Jesus then takes him aside to tell him something he does not tell the others, it cannot be that what he says is not intended for their ears as well. It is simply that, as Thomas tells them on returning, the way they would hear even one of the words he just heard would turn them against him. They would stone him as a common blasphemer.

The images of fire and water in this passage attract our attention. The very stones that would carry out the death sentence have a fire within them that would turn the judgment against the accusers and blister the hands that try to throw them. It is as if the fire that Jesus had cast on earth and is keeping watch over has entered into the very stones and would flare up to expose the ignorance of those who presume to understand. Jesus is also the custodian of the bubbling spring from which Thomas has drunk. It is not that Jesus has hidden it from the others. It is there for all, but only Thomas has stooped down to drink from it.

All of this makes it clear that the three words that Thomas hears in private are not meant for him alone. Like *all* the sayings of Jesus, they are secret only because the listeners choose not to hear them, or at least are not prepared to hear them. Hence we must not assume that the *Gospel* intends to reserve them for Thomas. At this point, we have only two hints as to what he might have said: first that the disciples are to understand themselves as children of the same living father (logion 3), and second, that since it is Judas the Twin who has recognized this, that they are to understand themselves in some sense also as the twins of Jesus. Although this is the first and last time that the person of Judas Thomas will appear in the *Gospel*, the image of the "twin of Jesus" will overshadow everything that is said from here on.

It is not without further irony that the two disciples who fail to understand Jesus' question about who he is are Peter and Matthew, the two figures who insisted on the primacy of Peter among the followers of Jesus. Thus not only has the counsel that they should follow James the Just been inverted; their allegiance to *any* of the organized communities is irrelevant. Let them follow both, but if they must follow one, let it be Thomas whose authority rests in having understood that there *is* no authority other than that of seeing and understanding for oneself.

---

14. Jesus said to them, "If you fast, you will bring sin upon yourselves; and, if you pray, you will be condemned; and if you give alms, you will do harm to your spirits. When you enter a land and wander through the district, if people receive you, eat whatever they set before you. Heal the sick among them. For that which goes in your mouth will not defile you; it is what comes out of your mouth that will defile you."

In order to tell the disciples the secrets that Thomas was afraid to tell them, Jesus needs to shake them further out of their old habits of thought, and this is what the present logion does in dramatic, almost exaggerated language. Among the Jews of Judea it was a considered a defilement to eat with gentiles and required that they be purified before observing religious customs. Jesus turns the idea on its head by considering it sinful *not* to forsake the observances and break the taboos.

It will not do to see Jesus as a simple outlaw or as exempt from ordinary religious observances in virtue of a higher authority. Having made it clear in so many words he does not wish to be seen as their Master, Jesus' admonition to the disciples cannot be understood as instructions to be followed on his authority. If there is anything that distinguishes the pure from the impure, it must be discovered from the inside out, not the other way around. These are not the kind of words that a disciple can understand by listening to an explanation, and Jesus does not offer one. The only way to know what he is talking about is to stand where he is standing when he speaks to them, and the only way to know if one is standing there is to speak from the heart and attend to what comes out of one's mouth. Gradually, step by step, we are coming to see that to be drawn into the text is to be drawn into an identification with *something* in Jesus that is secret only because it cannot be likened to anything that words can tell.

Despite the sin and condemnation Jesus here associates with the most ordinary and accepted of religious practices, he has already made it clear in logion 6 that his only intention to break their link to the kingdom. Thus, for example, there is nothing despicable in sharing what one has with those who are in need. But when it is identified as almsgiving the act is transformed from a simple giving into an act of piety or loyalty to tradition that gives it additional value that it would not otherwise have. It is the same with prayer and fasting. If such things are done begrudgingly and out of spite for what one desires, no matter how highly they are esteemed by social convention, they corrode the spirit. The place of life is not to be reached by custom and convention; as old and venerable as they are, they smack of death. And so when it comes to dietary laws, the disciples are advised when they wander into the countryside, far from the shadow of the temple, not to carry the ways of the temple around with them, but to eat what is put in front of them. For the kingdom is what *is* in front of you, not in what you *expect* to see there.

In this logion we have the first reference to healing in the *Gospel*. While Jesus is not himself presented as a miracle healer, that he should encourage healing just after having rejected other religious practices leaves no doubt that he is not referring to the miraculous cure of physical or mental ailments where someone serves as the agent, or angel, of some higher power. His is a different kind of healing because his is a different idea of sickness: the darkness of ignorance that needs to be exposed to the light. This is something no one can achieve in the place of anyone else. If I do not know myself, no one else can accomplish it for me. The kingdom may be hidden, but this does not mean that it is some kind of occult power that can be harnessed to change the fortunes of those around us. It is hidden because it is not seen. The manifestation, we have been told (logion 5), will take care of itself. The only healing to be done is to name the sickness; it is up to the listener to accept the diagnosis or not.

15. Jesus said, "When you see one who was not born of woman, fall on your face and worship him. That one is your father."

We have seen Jesus draw the attention of the disciples away from his own person and toward something as yet unknown, something that has to do with knowing oneself. Here we are given the most direct indication so far just what that might be, but the words are so surprising that one is forced to ask if they are really saying what, in the light of everything that has gone before, they seem to say: that we have a father who has no mother, that this father of ours can be seen by those who seek to know themselves, and that seeing will drive us to our knees in adoration.

In the mythical worldview of the disciples, Adam was the only person not born of woman, but Adam is neither visible nor worthy of adoration. Not even a symbolic Adam, a kind of "primordial human" residing in an eternal sphere from the beginning of time would qualify as the kind of father Jesus is talking about. And given everything that has been said about the kingdom being within us and right before our face (logion 3), we cannot imagine Jesus to be telling us here that this father of ours dwells in another, higher reality beyond the reach of our experience. No such idea of divinity has been suggested, nor will it be, in the *Gospel*. Only something unborn yet visible to those who know themselves can answer to the description Jesus gives.

It is as if we were being invited to see in ourselves something that Jesus is already aware of in himself. For this unborn father to dwell within would then make us twins of the living Jesus, children sharing one and the same living father. And if there is something *in us* that is unborn, then it is not a creation of the father but that very father himself, and we his children. This unborn father within is that which unifies us all—every soul of us on earth, Jesus included—into a kind of family of motherless twins. Having seen, we can only fall down on our faces in awe of what we have come to know about ourselves: we who are born of woman bear within us something unborn that our mothers could not give us, indeed that *no one* could give us because it is no one's to give. In effect, this creates a dual image of the human being, each one being a child *in time* and a father *out of time* at the same time. Now we understand the sense in which we need to see ourselves as divided into two (logion 11). I am who *I am* because I am also something *that is not I.* Knowing this about ourselves, we have to wonder what would become of our ordinary identity as individuals and the whole web of relationships that support it. Jesus anticipates the question in what he has to say next.

> *16. Jesus said, "People might think I have come to cast peace on the world. They do not know that I have come to cast dissension on the earth: fire, sword, war. For there will be five in a house: three will be set against two and two against three, father against son and son against father, and they will stand alone."*

Since it is the whole earth that Jesus takes as the object of his fire, sword, and war there is no indication that he is proposing to his disciples any kind of armed revolt—spiritually motivated or otherwise—in which they are to emerge victorious. The purpose is stated clearly: to create divisions everywhere so that in the end they can all stand alone. There is no reason to read into the text any covert reference to sexual abstinence as preferable to ordinary family life. The meaning is clear enough as it stands: To be united into something new we must first be disunited from our current relationships. The former household must fall apart for a new family to come to be. The ties between father and son must be broken so that each can stand alone. Jesus does not say that these divisions are meant to *isolate* individuals from one another or to *annihilate* the family unit. We must assume, in the absence of anything to the contrary, that the fire will one day return to the hearth, the sword to its sheath, and the war to peace. It is not wanton destruction that Jesus promotes but a new *integration* into a kingdom within oneself and without. It is just that the knot needs to be united before it can be retied.

At the same time, there is a sense in which the divisions Jesus means to incite *are* permanent. There is no talk of one side conquering or subduing the other. If the order he imagines is to be a place of life and not a static and unchanging realm beyond time and history, then it must be a place where each, standing alone, can rely on the other and in that reliance become one. Knowing the self, as was said in logion 3, entails being known. The relationship between Jesus and his disciples is not at that point; they have yet to be disengaged from their usual way of thinking and judging. The relation between Jesus and Thomas is different. They are twins precisely because each is able to stand alone, and they are able to stand alone because each knows himself as what he is and as what he is not. Each is a unique child of the unborn father they bear within, and are known as such by one another.

> *17. Jesus said, "I will give you what no eye has seen, what no ear has heard and no hand has touched, what has never arisen in the human heart."*

As we saw in logion 15, it is not Jesus' place to give us the unborn father; we already possess that as part of our human being. The fire he casts on the earth is only *his awareness* of that fact, a smoldering flame that it is up to his listeners to fan into a fire or let go out. In addition, this awareness is not an elevation to a state of mystical rapture but a recognition of what lies right in front of our face; the father that makes us twins, he said, is something we can see. Therefore, what he promises to give us in the words of this saying cannot be thought to lie beyond the senses, only beyond what we have so far been able to perceive with them. If that awareness is something to be seen and touched and heard, and not merely something that can be believed or meditated on in the heart of man, then the knowledge Jesus is talking of will involve not only a new understanding but a restoration of our sight, our hearing, and our touch so that they can see what has so far been hidden from them. What illumines the mind must also heighten the senses. How could a kingdom in which we have become one with what is within us and without, in which we rule over all, be a place of life if we were disembodied spirits?

> *18. The disciples said to Jesus, "Tell us how our end will be."*
> *Jesus said, "Have you found the beginning that you search for the end? For where the beginning is, there the end will be. Blessed is the one who will stand at the beginning. That one will know the end and will not taste death."*

The unrepentant folly of the disciples' questions, like this one, is not only meant to contrast with the radical nature of Jesus' answers. They also serve to show, again and again, how the reason the words of Jesus are secret is that something in the listener prevents them from understanding what is being said. The reader who is engaged in this tug-of-war over the meaning of the words is thus brought face to face with the choice of being an obstinate and dim-witted disciple or a Thomas, one who seeks in order to receive an answer to the questions one sets out with or one who seeks without any bias toward what there is to be found at the end.

That said, it is not hard to sympathize with the disciples' point of view. After all, these are persons who have left their families and professions, and are naturally eager to know how long this journey with Jesus can be expected to go on and what it will all lead to. Jesus' answer disavows that sympathy entirely, accusing his questioners of not even having begun. He is simply not interested in the end. What is to be sought is to be sought here and now, without concern for whether we actually find it or not. We will only know what is to be found when it has found us, and there is no greater obstacle to that knowledge than preoccupation with the object of the search. The deliverance from death of which Jesus speaks does not, therefore, refer to some other realm beyond our own. It is a result of what is known by the living. Not to taste death is to have found the unborn, after which everything tastes alive.

> *19. Jesus said, "Blessed is one who came into being before coming into being. If you become my disciples and listen to my words, these stones will serve you. For there are five trees in paradise that do not change in summer or winter and do not shed their leaves. Whoever knows them will not taste death."*

This logion ends the same as the last, and should therefore be read as a further comment on its final words about a knowing that does not taste death. The first phrase appears to be an enigma, but the solution has already been presented in the image of the unborn father we met in logion 15. Who can be before coming into being? Since the answer cannot lie in a transcendent realm beyond the world but must be right before our face, we need to understand the question to mean: What is it *in me* that is apart from what *I* have come to be? As we saw in the previous logion, it is something death cannot touch.

We were already told of stones that seem to serve Jesus and Thomas, by catching fire and burning any who tried to cast them in condemnation against one who sees what Jesus has seen (logion 13). Here the same service of the stones is promised to those who hear the words of Jesus and become his disciples. Obviously, he does not yet consider those whom the text refers to as his "disciples" to qualify as such, presumably because they still think in terms of stoning what they do not understand rather than accept the fire that Jesus is offering them to shed light on the bias in their understanding. Here, as before, there is nothing magical about the promise of power over stones. It is rather another instance of the way Jesus inverts our ordinary way of thinking. Those who act out of the darkness of ignorance *seem* to be in control of their judgments, whereas in fact it is their judgments that are in control of them. The way to regain the control and have the stones serve *us* is to learn what Jesus has learned.

The statement about the five trees in paradise that neither shed their leaves nor change with the seasons is clearly meant to be connected with being served by the stones. If we accept that image as having to do with regaining control over our judgments, then the meaning of this new image is illumined: they represent the fulfillment of the promise in logion 17 to restore the savor of life to the senses.

Judgments based on illusory dichotomies are like self-fulfilling prophecies. Insofar as the categories on which they are based remain in the dark, every judgment confirms the validity of every other. And as these categories work their way into our language and social customs, they not only infect the way we think about the world but also the way we perceive it. To return to the image in logion 4, the nostalgia the old man feels for the detached and immediate sensuality of the infant of seven days is a result of knowing what to expect of our senses and having become all but anesthetized to fresh experiences.

To see through our judgments to the habits of thought that lie behind them is also, therefore, to see through the routine way we have come to use the senses. Awakening of the mind is not complete without an awakening of the body.

The image of five trees in paradise offsets that of the tree of the knowledge of what is good and what is evil that was said to stand in the middle of the Garden of Eden. The saying speaks of them not as part of a lost, primeval paradise but as something we have, just as we already know that we have the tree of knowledge as part of our human legacy. If we see these five trees as an image of the five senses, then they, too, are in need of awakening and restoration as much as are our dark and twisted habits of separating good from evil. That they are set in paradise where they are forever in bloom seems to tell us that our bodies share in the dual nature of being what we are before we came to be what we now are. There is something in the senses that is forever unborn in them, something that can be restored. In that sense, the only dualism there can be between a mortal body and an immortal spirit is one generated in ignorance of our true natures.

> 20. *The disciples said to Jesus, "Tell us, what is the kingdom of heaven like?"*
>
> *He said to them, "It is like a mustard seed. It is the smallest of all seeds, but when it falls on plowed soil, it produces a great plant and becomes a shelter for the birds of the sky."*

The phrase kingdom of heaven is not Jesus' but that of his disciples. In his reply, he explains further what he had said earlier about the place of life where each one is the center and rules over all. It is, he says, like a farmer planting a single mustard seed and cultivating it. The irony of the parable would not have been lost on his listeners. His kingdom is not cultivated but grows wild, like the mustard weed. Every farmer among them who would have tried cultivating it from the smallest of all seeds (at least of all *planted* seeds) knows how hard it is to control and keep from spreading. They would also have known that even the largest of mustard plants hardly offers a suitable place for the birds of the sky to nest. In other words, the parable means precisely the opposite of what it says. The kingdom *cannot* be tended and controlled as if were just another social establishment, and it *does not* offer refuge from the world that is all around us, since it is there that the kingdom is. It is like a mustard seed: it spreads without a care for what we expect of it and is always exposed to everything under heaven. Its home is in its homelessness.

21. Mary said to Jesus, "What are your disciples like?"

He said, "They are like little children who have settled in a field that is not theirs. When the owners of the field come and say, 'Give us our field,' they undress before them in order to let them have their field back, and they return the field. Therefore I say, if the owner of a house knows that a thief is coming, he will stand watch before he arrives and will not let him break into his house of his estate and carry away his goods. As for you, be on your guard against the world. Arm yourselves with great strength lest the robbers find a way to get to you, for the trouble you expect will surely come.

"Let there be in your midst one who understands. When the crop ripened, he came quickly, sickle in hand, and harvested. Whoever has ears to hear, let them hear."

This saying contains an ambiguity about whether the woman identified only as Mary is among the disciples or not. If she is, then the question she is asking has to do with Jesus' idea of what a disciple *should* be. If she is not, it could be a simple question about what his disciples are *in fact* like, a question that could well contain a little sarcasm given their responses to what Jesus is saying. In either case, the question follows naturally from Jesus' request of his listeners to make themselves disciples, and his answer is clearly what he *expects* them to be like. The admonitions in the second half of the saying are therefore addressed to everyone who would be a disciple. That said, we need to keep in mind that in rejecting the title of master (logion 13), Jesus has already implicitly rejected the correlative category of disciple.

His reply begins with two images, both about expropriating someone else's territory. In the first, the children take over a field; in the second, the householder is on the watch against thieves. The context of everything that comes before and follows this logion makes it clear that the purpose of the intrusions has nothing to do with material goods; it has to do with the tug-of-war over ways of thinking. Both the things that we are made to believe as members of a particular society and the questions that are raised about those beliefs have to do with the ordering or reordering of one's house.

The children who have taken over a field that is not theirs are in the open air—neither have they been completely housed in conventional thinking nor have they built a house of their own. But insofar as they are still children, by that very fact they are trespassers moving freely in and out of the established social boundaries. When they are chased away, they not only return the field to the state it was in before they had invaded it with their childishness, they return the clothes that also, somehow, belong to the field. The image could hardly be clearer: when criticized for disrupting social habits, they opt to remain children, shedding even the few habits they have. This is what Jesus understands by making oneself a disciple.

The meaning of the second image is now clearer. Breaking into a house and looting it is different from walking onto someone else's field. A house is better protected. As disciples, one is both a thief and a custodian. To break into the house of conventions and reappropriate what is there as one's own and to guard one's own house against the intrusions of the world require discipline. Each protects its territory and is anxious to overtake the others. Mere awareness of the kingdom offers no more protection than the mustard plant offers to the birds of the air. One needs the wisdom of the world as well.

In the alternating role we are assigned of custodian and thief, we have the first clear indication, already hinted at before, of a double-entendre in the notion of the world. On the one hand, it means everything under heaven, the visible world of nature as well as the invisible world of the spirit. This is the sole locus of the kingdom but it is also the recipient of the fire that Jesus brings. It is the place of life and the setting for self-understanding, and at the same time it is impoverished and clouded over by the darkness of ignorance. Only occasionally in the *Gospel* are these two meanings separated; more often, they entail one another.

The admonition to attach oneself to a person who understands is a way of admitting that discipleship is fostered best in the presence of those who can serve as guides, those who know when the period of ripening has ended and it is time to harvest. One does not recognize a ripened crop instinctively. One has to be shown by those with experience, who in turn had to be shown by someone else. Jesus seems here not only to be begging for acceptance in that role himself, but perhaps also to be reinforcing his earlier advice to the disciples that they align themselves with Thomas (logion 13). The final comment here—and from here on throughout the *Gospel*—amounts to a kind of exclamation mark, marking the end of what Jesus says and the beginning at which the listeners are asked, Then what will you do (logion 11)?

> 22. *Jesus saw some infants nursing. He said to his disciples, "These nursing infants are like those who enter the kingdom."*
>
> *They said to him, "Shall we then enter the kingdom as infants?"*
>
> *Jesus said to them, "When you make the two one, when you make the inner as the outer and the outer as the inner and the upper as the lower, and when you make the male and the female into a single one, so that the male will not be male nor the female be female, when you make an eye in the place of an eye, a hand in the place of a hand, a foot in the place of a foot, and an image in the place of an image, then you will enter."*

Here we are given further elaboration of what it is that we, advanced in years, have to learn from the suckling infant, the child of seven days (logion 4). The oblique reference to the restoration of the senses is here made explicit. The body that we have been accustomed to ordering around as a master does a servant—the eyes, the feet, the hands that have become mere appendages need to be reappropriated and restored to the original state of the infant child who sees and touches the world as a single one with it. In restoring the senses one also restores the mind and heart, in a way that only an adult who *becomes* a child can. To know oneself is to refresh also the image one has of the world, to replace what habits see with what is in fact manifest all around us. It is not enough to see what the kingdom is like; we must also *see through* the likenesses to what it *is*. So, too, with the question of what it means to be a disciple: it means breaking through the illusory dichotomy of disciple and Master to recognize oneself as nothing less than the twin of Jesus. Only then can we understand the reason why the enlightened opposition between within and without, up and down, male and female does not consist in melting them into one or favoring one at the expense of the other. The two need to be integrated as opposing realities that need each other to be complete.

> *23. Jesus said, "I shall choose you, one from a thousand, and two from ten thousand, and they will stand as a single one."*

Simple arithmetic tells us that in these words Jesus is saying that the larger the group, the fewer the chosen. Since we already know that the secrecy of the sayings is intended for all, there can be no question of elitism intended. It is also clear that in no sense can discipleship refer to a "race" of chosen ones or to a mass of persons identified by any particular tradition of beliefs. Jesus' choice is simply an indication of his preference for those who themselves choose to stand as solitary ones rather than for those who follow him out of obligation to a group will. Election is a *consequence* of understanding, not a *precondition* for it.

> *24. His disciples said, "Show us the place where you are, for we must seek it."*
>
> *He said to them, "Whoever has ears to hear, let them hear. There is light within a person of light and it lights up the whole world. When it does not shine, there is darkness."*

At last the disciples ask the kind of question that Jesus expects them to ask, or at least he understands it in that fashion: to stand in the place where he can stand to say what he says. The place Jesus offers them is the place of light within that transforms them into persons of light that illumine the entire world about them. It is not enough to locate some *part* of the world to inhabit in the enjoyment of self-knowledge; one must also be known everywhere as a true solitary (logion 3) who illumines the whole of the world and dispels darkness wherever he walks.

> *25. Jesus said, "Love your brother like your soul; guard him like the apple of your eye."*

The mandate to love one's brother as one's own soul implies that one first love one's own soul. To love out of duty is a contradiction in terms and discloses a deep distrust of oneself. To love ourselves we must know ourselves, in our entirety, just as we are. Only then will our sight be restored so that the true image of the other that is reflected in our eye is received as a pupil or little child, without prejudice or expectation, and watched over with the same care with which we watch over what is most precious to us. To stand in the place where Jesus stands and see what he sees in his disciples that they do not yet even see in themselves (logion 24) requires a transformation in the way we know ourselves.

> *26. Jesus said, "The chip that is in your brother's eye you see, but the log in your own eye you do not see. When you take the log out of your eye, then you will see to remove the chip from your brother's eye."*

If one does not love oneself—which means refusing to do what one hates to do (logion 6)—one has driven a log through the eye that distorts our view of everyone around us and inhibits the light within us from illuminating the world without us. The fact that Jesus refers to that impediment to seeing as a log suggests that it is not the petty social customs that are the problem, but something in the very structure of the house of conventional wisdom itself. No ethic based on rules or customs, however powerful, can awaken one to the needs of another as self-knowledge can do.

27. *"If you do not fast from the world, you will not find the kingdom; if you do not keep the sabbath a sabbath, you will not see the father."*

The world we are asked to fast from is the very world in which fasting is carried out as a matter of religious obligation or for personal merit (logion 6) because it precludes discovery of the world in which the kingdom is manifest. The fasting Jesus is speaking of is a refusal to take in the social categories and ways of thinking that are set before us. It can hardly be accomplished by conformity to dietary laws or by refusal to eat food that is offered to us by others who have different eating customs (logion 14).

So, too, the sabbath is not to be *respected* out of a sense of tradition as if it were a commandment imposed from without with respect to one day of the week. It is to be celebrated as the companion of every day of the week. If the sabbath is a day of rest, then rest is something that belongs to our everyday. Although we must live daily within the conventional world, we are being advised also and at the same time take a rest from the world.

28. *Jesus said, "I stood in the midst of the world and appeared to them in the flesh. I found them all drunk and none of them thirsting. My soul ached for the children of humanity, because they are blind in their hearts and do not see that they came empty into the world and seek to go out*

*of the world empty. But now they are drunk. When they
have shaken off their wine, then they shall repent."*

Although it is the ordinary world in which Jesus says he
has taken his stand, the speaker here is not the ordinary Jesus
and his words make us want to back up and review everything
that was said so far. It is his "alter ego," the father, who speaks
through him. Still, it *is* the same Jesus, but the change of voice
alerts us to his "alter ego" who speaks whenever Jesus speaks.
It is a kind of voice behind the voice the disciples are fixed
on, an echo that reverberates and gives depth to his language.
This is where Jesus stands and where he invited his disciples to
stand, if only they can become integrated, solitary ones. It is
the place where that which is by nature one and that which one
has become are one. The unborn speaks through Jesus without
him ceasing to be the man Jesus.

At the same time, the clear reference to the flesh removes
any lingering down about the living Jesus as being a mere
appearance or about the fulfillment of the search coming in
dimension beyond this world.

Earlier we heard Jesus chide Thomas for being inebriated with the recognition that he and Jesus are spiritual twins
(logion 13). Here we understand better the reason for the rep-
rimand: drunkenness takes away thirst and hence blurs one's
vision; one is too disoriented to have the will to search. But
this is only a temporary condition, not the permanent state of
a "fallen nature." This is evident from the fact that Jesus speaks
from a position of sobriety and exclaims that his heart aches
for those who are not. Jesus' role as teacher is to set them back
on the search, not to find anything *for* them, and certainly not
to correct a birth defect. The problem is not that the children
of humanity are wicked but that they are blind in their hearts.

Once they shake off their wine, they will be free to see more clearly. The Coptic text ends with the transliteration of the Greek word *metanoia*. The repentance it is meant to describe is not an admission of guilt or even a making of amends for wrongs committed, but simply a sobering up. Drunkenness is an intoxication of knowledge, a darkening ignorance. As infants, we come into the world empty, with the potential to be filled up with light and in turn to enlighten the world about us. The heartache is that so many leave the world as empty as they entered it, sodden with the same cheap wine as those who prefer illusions to the place of life.

> *29. Jesus said, "If the flesh came into being because of spirit, it is a marvel; but if spirit came into existence because of the body, it is a marvel of marvels. Indeed, I am amazed at how such great wealth has made its home in such poverty."*

Having already announced his own bodily presence in the world as itself a kind of revelation, it is not surprising to hear him affirm spirit and flesh as correlative ideas. Clearly flesh refers to the body and the whole of sensual experience. Spirit is an equally general term, lacking any hint of a doctrine of a higher dimension of immortality beyond this world. In the context of the *Gospel* it can only refer to knowledge, emotions, and everything we speak of metaphorically as within us. It is from this perspective that Jesus sees flesh serving to manifest spirit as a marvel, and spirit manifesting flesh as an even greater marvel.

Applied to the previous logion, this would suggest that there is something more wondrous about Jesus than the fact that his spirit is revealed in the flesh—the fact that his spirit is a revelation of what is already present, but hidden, in the flesh. Not only does this completely unravel the idea of spirit as primordially disembodied, it suggests that the restoration of the senses referred to earlier is actually a positive spiritualizing of the flesh. The poverty he refers to is not the inferiority of the flesh vis-à-vis the richness of the spirit. Here poverty has nothing to do with material poverty, ascetic renunciation, or the casting off of the body. It is not a question of something lacking to the flesh or of a superabundance of spirit. In the context of this *Gospel*, as we have already seen (logion 3), it is the state of not knowing oneself and hence not being able to be known. The real mystery, then, is that our very ignorance contains within itself the seed of a great richness, an integration that depends on the eternal, mutually enriching struggle of flesh and spirit.

Lest we read anything cosmic into this struggle, we need to remember that in the *Gospel*, awareness of being divided is a precondition for becoming one. We need see nothing more in the struggle between flesh and spirit than the "split vision" of seeing the world from two standpoints at one and the same time. It is as if the world looked differently when seen with the right eye than it does when seen with the left, but in both cases the depth of perception is lost. To view the world with both eyes open would be to overcome the dichotomy, but our condition is such that this full and perfect vision comes only in flashes, moments of illumination when we are fully awake.

30. Jesus said, "Where there are three gods, they are gods; where there are two or one, I am with that person."

To grasp the meaning of this logion, we do best to begin from the apparent grammatical contradiction of the final sentence. The one or two whom Jesus is with refers to the solitary, the one in whom the two are integrated; it is one *and* two. The parables aside, whenever Jesus talks in the *Gospel* about what he expects of his disciples, it is always about "he," the individual, the solitary; when he talks about what is lacking, he talks in the plural, about people, "they." The solitary is a distinct individual and at the same time the locus of the unborn father in virtue of which he and Jesus are truly twins. If that father is thought of only as a deity inhabiting another world, then his place is with the gods, a kind of divine "they" who belong primarily to each other. Only if the person is aware of himself as a duality of father and individual, or as an integrated oneness of the two, is it possible for the living Jesus to be with him, that is, to be his twin. Here, as always, knowledge of oneself is a prerequisite to discovering the kingdom of twins. As for the idea of a single transcendent God, the single most important belief in the Jewish tradition, Jesus has nothing to say in the *Gospel*.

31. Jesus said, "A prophet is not acceptable in the prophet's own village; a doctor does not heal those who know the doctor."

Jesus is not only talking about himself from his own experience. He is telling us more about what he expects of a disciple. Having already told his listeners to think of themselves as healers (logion 14) whose task is to enlighten the world about them (logion 24), it is not hard to see why those in darkness should reject the prophet as no more than another member of their own town, or to resist the diagnosis of their illness because they think they know the doctor. But just as one cannot expect to be known without first knowing oneself, so too those who do not recognize their own ignorance mistake the light for darkness.

32. Jesus said, "A city built on a high mountain and fortified
cannot fall, nor can it be hidden."

The fortified city, like the house that is protected against
the intruder (logion 16), does not stand strong because it hides
itself from the scrutiny of the world. Occult teachings intended
for a small elite of savants protect themselves by obscurity of
language and secret codes. Secret sayings intended to be cast
upon the world draw strength from standing in the light and
are able to resist assault by the very fact that they are too much
in evidence to deny. In this sense, the words of Jesus suggest
his conviction that the more manifest the light of insight, the
less chance it has of being swallowed up by the darkness of
ignorance. His faith in the innate desire of human nature to *see*
could not be clearer: what is visible is invincible.

33. Jesus said, "What you hear in your ear, proclaim in the
other ear from your housetops. For no one kindles a lamp
and puts it under a basket, nor does one put it in a hid-
den place. One sets it on a lamp stand so that everyone who
comes and goes will see its light."

In logion 22 we were told to come to a new awareness of
our eyes and hands and feet. The same point is reiterated here
in slightly different fashion. The two ears we are told to use
in order to hear are not the two amplifiers attached to either
side of our head. These are the outer *ear* that simply picks
up sounds. Only by listening with the *inner* ear can we hear
what bears proclaiming from the housetops. Just as light, once
exposed, shines of its own for all to see, so true insight cannot
shine inside of one without expressing itself outwardly. Once
again the idea of a hidden meaning in the sayings is repudiated
in unambiguous language.

34. Jesus said, "If a blind person leads a blind person, the two of them fall into a pit."

Commonplace as this proverb is, it has another purpose for being included here. First, it contrasts the power of the light that has been uncovered with impotence and unreliability of darkness. Second, those who are themselves blind cannot know that they are being guided, or rather misguided, by persons who are equally blind. Like the drunkard (logion 28), the blind person is disoriented and needs the guidance of those whose eyes are opened (logion 21), not of those who direct one to the kingdom where it is not (logion 3). Those who are ignorant of their own blindness and yet presume to lead others are no better than one who tries to remove the sliver in the eye of another without seeing the log in his own (logion 26).

35. Jesus said, "It is impossible for one to enter the house of someone strong and take it by force without tying that person's hands. Then one can loot the house."

Here we have the complement to logion 32, which told us how to fortify and protect our own house. We are told that in order to overcome a house and loot it of its belongings, we need to incapacitate the powerful who protect it. The problem is not that the house constructed of conventions, laws, customs, and religious observances is empty of all meaning, but rather that its meaning has been expropriated and taken out of our hands. To appropriate it as our own, we must bind the hands of the wrongful owners, just as the fire that would illumine must consume something in the process.

Far from advising us to cling passively to our own insight, to strip off the habits of the world and skip away naked and content like little children, he advises us to return fortified

and to take back, by force, what is rightfully ours. It is only the
house fortified by the light and having nothing to hide, the
house that belongs to all and to none, that is to be considered
a place of life.

> *36. Jesus said, "Do not be anxious from morning to evening
> and from evening to morning about what you will wear."*

To see through one's habits is to be detached from them.
To know what social customs and conventional ways of thinking can do and what they cannot frees one from preoccupation
with dressing in fashion or out of fashion. We cannot walk
around in society naked; we need to be able to communicate
and to interact with others. But we can walk around dressed
in conventions knowing all the while that there is no shame
in being naked and no dignity in dressing one way or another.
Knowing oneself, there is nothing to hide (logion 5) and no
reason to fret over how to dress it up. The light can only shine
through habits that have become transparent to those who
wear them. This is said to be as true of waking experience from
morning to night as it is of sleeping experience from night to
morning, as if knowing oneself required even liberating us
from the way we think about and value the dreams and visions
that visit us in the half-light of repose.

> *37. His disciples said, "When will you be revealed to us and
> when will we see you?"*
> *Jesus said, "When you undress without being ashamed,
> and you take your clothes and put them under your feet like
> little children and trample on them, then you will see the
> son of the living one and you will not be afraid."*

Despite having heard Jesus tell them that he has already
revealed himself to them in living flesh (logion 28), his

disciples act as if he were not standing before them and ask when they will see him revealed. Jesus discards the foolishness of the request by playing on their own words and elaborating further what he has just finished saying. Just as he had first responded to the question about religious observances by advising his listeners to avoid doing anything that their heart is not in (logion 8) and later condemned them as sinful (logion 14), here he adds force to his counsel to doff one's clothes (logion 21) by telling us to trample on them like little children. Only in so doing can one overcome the fear of nakedness that prevents us from recognizing in Jesus the voice of the living one and in themselves the sons of the living one that it is theirs to become by understanding his words.

There is no indication here of a return to the paradisal state of Adam and Eve. As we have seen again and again, wherever Jesus relies on mythical stories or doctrines of tradition, he does so explicitly, not by implication. The engagement demanded of the reader is never to detect which images refer to which parts of traditional belief, but to understand the fundamental question. At the same time, questions assuming that there is something unique about Jesus are always deflected as wide of the mark. His answers work rather to stimulate a transformation of perspective without which the questioners can never see themselves the way Jesus sees them, as his twins by birth.

38. Jesus said, "Many times you desired to hear these words I am saying to you, and you have no one else from whom to hear them. There will be days when you will seek me, and you will not find me."

Jesus recognizes in this saying the willingness of his disciples to listen to him and accepts the fact that he is the only one around them to whom they can turn. At the same time, he warns them that his time with them is limited. There is another message: if they fail to understand, the fault is not his but falls squarely at the feet of his disciples. The allusion to seeking and not finding once again confirms the secondary place of the messenger, who comes and goes, vis-à-vis the kingdom, which is always there. So regularly do the disciples miss both the meaning of the message and the role of the messenger that we have to think the *Gospel* introduces them for no other reason than to highlight the radical nature of what Jesus has to say.

If we look at the pattern emerging in their questions, we see that they are prone to understand customs and observances as the core of religion, that they revere tradition as unassailable, that they are anxious to know what lies on the other side of death, and that they expect a Messiah whom they suspect may be Jesus—all things that Jesus explicitly rejects.

> *39. Jesus said, "The Pharisees and the scribes have taken the keys of knowledge and hidden them. They did not enter themselves, nor have they allowed those who wish to enter to do so. As for you, be wise as serpents and as innocent as doves."*

The keys of knowledge need to be appropriated as much as all conventional knowledge received from the past, but the fact that they are deliberately hidden only make the appropriation all the more difficult. It gives them an aura of sacredness or truth that they do not deserve. The contrast with the secret sayings announced in the incipit to this *Gospel* is obvious, giving us once again the deliberate ambivalence of language that only engagement in the text can clear up. The sayings of the *Gospel* are open for all to know and only become sacred when they have been known, whereas the secret oral tradition of the Pharisees is rejected as a means to control what is known. Their codes of interpretation are only the illusion of control, which makes them no better than the blind leading the blind. What separates the scribes and Pharisees from the disciples is that the disciples are on the receiving end and therefore freer to shake free of that illusion than those whose identity depends on the illusion. Hence the concluding comment.

The combination of opposites—the cleverness of the serpent and the innocence of the dove—provides the same sort of paradox we met in the image of the city on the mountaintop whose invincibility lies in its accessibility to all. The serpent crawls on the earth and the dove flies in the skies, but the two must become one, the above like the below. In other words, it is not enough to be a serpent sometimes and a dove at others. The serpent must be innocent and the dove become clever. The tug-of-war over the meaning of the words and symbols on which tradition depends requires as much.

40. Jesus said, "A vine was planted outside of the father and did not grow strong. It will be pulled up by its roots and left to rot."

To be apart from the father means for one to cultivate oneself as an individual defined by a single history and wrapped in a single bodily skin, ignoring the unborn father within that makes one a twin of every other vine on the stock. If we read this verse with the former, it is clear that the "they" who pull up the vine by its roots are none other than the keepers of tradition. The way to avoid being uprooted is to know oneself not only as a person in control of one's own life and destiny but as one who has been planted, by one's very nature, in something greater, the father. The mere individual on its own is no match for the power and authority of tradition; the solitary in touch with the unborn is in touch with the very root and lifeblood of tradition.

> *41. Jesus said, "Whoever who has something in hand will be given more; and whoever has nothing, even the little that person has will be taken away."*

The paradox in this saying is a result of the assumption that what I have in hand and is being increased or taken away from me are my own possessions to begin with. If we read this logion as a continuation of the former, we see that there is a sense in which one who has *appropriated* the knowledge of belonging to something greater than oneself differs from the one who simply acquiesces to control by the knowledge of those in authority. Appropriated knowledge cannot be taken from me or withheld in secrecy from me because it is not something *I have* but something that *has me*. In effect, we have a reversal of power taking place: the first who hold the keys are seen to be the last in terms of self-knowledge. Control of others decreases insight even as it inflates the illusion of insight.

> *42. Jesus said, "Be passers-by."*

To be a passer-by adds an important element to the earlier injunctions to be a seeker and a thirster, namely the call to homelessness. There is no indication that the *Gospel* is inviting disciples of Jesus to disengage themselves from all involvement in the world. Quite the contrary, liberation from conventional thinking is incomplete without a new illumination of the world (logion 24). If all things pass away (logion 11) refers to the impermanence of our every idea and image of the world, then we must be prepared to release ourselves from detachment to those ideas and refuse to domesticate ourselves in the house of the world. The inner house we are to build (logion 21) has no roof and no walls. It is everywhere precisely because it is bound to nowhere. The itinerant does not worry about dressing in fashion (logion 36) or simply seeking refuge in a kingdom located far beyond the world (logion 21). At the same time, to be a passer-by does not mean to view everything *sub specie mortis*, as if every enjoyment, every experience of life would leave a taste of death in one's mouth (logion 1). On the contrary, detachment enables us to taste life more to the full than attachment to customs, habits, and fashions does.

> *43. His disciples said to him, "Who are you to say these things to us?"*
>
> *"You do not know who I am from what I say to you but have become like the Jews. They either love the tree and hate the fruit, or they love the fruit and hate the tree."*

Having seen their religious leaders belittled, the disciples want to know by what authority Jesus speaks. They are setting up a decision between sources of authority in order to know which to follow. The answer undercuts the question by disposing, once again, of the authority of a teacher as a basis for self-understanding. It sets up in its place another choice between opposites that cannot be integrated because they are at the level at which the very nature of a true decision is distinguished from a false one.

Having said that a prophet is not accepted in his own country (logion 31), it is natural to reject as false any distinction between a prophet and what he says. The important thing, as we saw in logion 14, is not to ask where Jesus alone can stand so that we can trust in him, but to seek the place of life from which he speaks. Accordingly, the dichotomy between the fruit and the tree, which he attributed to the Judean authorities—not an ethnic appellation but a religious one aimed at those who guide astray (logion 3)—is illusory because the only way to know that the fruit is good is to become the tree and produce it oneself.

One can read a certain irony in the text in failing to identify the speaker explicitly as Jesus. The very question of the disciples elicits a voice from behind the question, as if the answer were already received but not yet accepted. The question they ask of Jesus reiterates the question they put to Thomas earlier (logion 13), who refused to reply on the grounds that they would have considered him a blasphemer. Jesus takes up the point directly in the following logion, inviting them to recognize what is really happening in their judgment of blasphemy.

> 44. *Jesus said, "One who blasphemes the father will be forgiven, and one who blasphemes the son will be forgiven. But one who blasphemes the holy spirit will not be forgiven, either on earth or in heaven."*

The *Gospel* tells us to recognize ourselves as sons of the living father (logion 3) and that to understand Jesus we have to see him as such a son (saying 37). Blasphemies against the father and the son are said to be forgivable, and those against the holy spirit not, but by *whom?* Surely not by Jesus himself. He can only be referring in the first instance to the religious authorities whom he has been consistently accusing of a failure to understand. Insofar as he is acceptable as a prophet, we have just heard, his claim to speak in the name of a higher authority should also be acceptable. What has happened, however, is they alternate between condemning him and condemning what he said, between hating the fruit of his words and hating the tree of the father in whose voice he speaks, shifting from one foot to the other in identifying what is blasphemy.

But to grant him *and* his words a position of authority is a sin too great to countenance. Jesus himself has already committed what in their eyes would be the unforgivable sin (logion 15) of replacing established religious authority by encouraging his disciples to see themselves, with him, as representing a new source of truth. He will not be forgiven by "them" any more than the disciples will if they stand where he stands and speak from their hearts the words he is speaking. It is the very authority to judge what is a sin of blasphemy and what is not that is called into question.

In this way, Jesus redefines the holy spirit as something holy in the human spirit and therefore repudiates the categories of sin seen through the eyes of the heaven and earth that will pass away. Such things, he has said in unambiguous terms, only do harm to our spirits (logion 14). This conventional wisdom must be passed by and seen through in order to understand what Thomas understood: that we are all born motherless twins of the same unborn father.

> *45. Jesus said, "Grapes are not harvested from thorns, nor figs from thistles, for these do not produce fruit. A good person brings forth good from the storehouse; a bad person brings forth evil from the evil storehouse of the heart and speaks evil things. Out of the abundance of the heart does such a person bring forth evil things."*

The same criticism that is raised against those who accept the fruit but reject the tree is repeated here as if to parry again the charge of blasphemy and, indirectly, invite them to reconsider the choice against following Thomas into the secrecy of the sayings. The tree itself cannot be eaten except through its fruit, just as the fruit produced by a vine that is cut off no longer manifests the life of the stalk (logion 40). So, too, the individual is not the unborn father but its manifestation in the flesh. We know Jesus by his words, but we only know ourselves by our own words. If all we know of ourselves is what we have been made to believe by those who guide us, our words are no more than the overflow of accepted conventions lodged in our hearts. If we know that we are what we are because of what we are not, we illumine the world as manifestations of the fullness of what we are.

The kingdom that is within us and all around us lies dormant like the fruit that lies hidden in the secret life of the tree. The only true blasphemy is to deny that holy spirit manifestation in the flesh of time and history.

> 46. *Jesus said, "From Adam to John the Baptist, among those born of women, no one is so great as John the Baptist that one's eyes should not be lowered in his presence. But I have said that whoever among you becomes a child will know the kingdom and will be greater than John."*

Jesus both praises his own teacher and supersedes his teachings, implying that the same is to be done to him by *his* disciples. Eyes lowered in respect for one's teacher need to be raised up in virtue of that which is higher than the teacher: that which no woman on earth can give birth to because it is unborn. That which distinguishes us from one another as children of our mothers gives us our identity as individuals but is not absolute and is not complete. That which unites us as motherless twins of the same father relativizes those distinctions, making it possible for us to become what the *Gospel* calls solitaries. Insofar as we are twins, we recognize ourselves as permanent infants as it were, constantly sustained in life by something that is always at the moment of birth, and in so knowing ourselves know the kingdom of which Jesus is speaking.

47. Jesus said, "A person cannot mount two horses or stretch two bows. A servant cannot serve two masters without honoring the one and offending the other. No one drinks old wine and immediately wants to drink new wine. New wine is not poured into old wineskins lest they burst; and aged wine is not poured into new wineskins lest it spoil. An old patch is not sewn onto a new garment, because it would tear away."

As we have seen, the discovery of ourselves as both born and unborn does not set up a split within our persons, such that one or the other aspect has to lord it over the other. It sets up the opposing dimensions of our humanity without which we cannot be whole. This integration cannot be brought about by exchanging one set of habits of mind and heart for another, as one were changing old clothes for new, or bringing oneself into fashion by discarding what has fallen out of line with the ruling norms. It requires rather breaking through these simple and crippling dichotomies in order to reach the true and living duality that we are by nature. To be complete, we need to get back in touch with what we love and refuse to act against it in the name of any authority on earth or heaven (logion 6).

This logion recapitulates the warning against defining ourselves in terms of conventional wisdom by means of a series of familiar proverbial sayings. By their nature, proverbs are contextual. Their truth is not in the nature of unchanging principles but in the concrete situation to which they speak, which is why it is so easy to counter any proverb with its opposite. In the *Gospel*, such proverbs serve much the same function as the use of double-meaning terms whose import changes according to the circumstances. Here the proverbial sayings are all pointed at the incompatibility of the awakened mind that has come to know itself with the subservience of the mind that has accommodated itself to social expectations. One cannot be of two minds on this matter any more than an archer can draw two bows or a rider mount two horses at the same time. One who has tasted knowledge like a fine aged wine cannot turn around and savor the mere illusion of knowledge. If one puts that aged wine into new wineskins, it will sour just as good knowledge will go bad if poured into the categories of current opinion. And if one puts new wine in fine aged wineskins, its immaturity will burst them. One could as well reverse the reference of the imagery and say that when new wine is poured into old wineskins that are inflexible and can no longer expand with the wine, what is still living in the new wine will burst through the skins that were only suited to what had all but stopped living. Finally, just as a new garment when washed shrinks and tears away from an old patch, so one cannot use old ideas to enhance or repair new ones.

The repetition of several proverbs one after the other, in terms that are ambiguous as to reference, has a single point: to achieve integrity as a human being, one cannot inhabit two opposing worldviews at the same time. In the end, one has to choose between the kingdom that is all around or the kingdom of the skies, between the world of conventional habit and the world illuminating and illumined by self-knowledge.

> 48. Jesus said, *"If two make peace between themselves in the same house, they shall say to the mountain, 'Move away,' and it will move."*

Here we are told something more about the new house that replaces the house of conventions, the house that does not separate but unites. The two that are said to make peace here are the same two that must at the same time remain in eternal conflict, defining one another and illumining all around them, namely, the born and the unborn. This is not a mere cessation of hostilities or a truce among equals guaranteeing noninterference. It is the peace of the solitary whose integrity is living because of the opposites it makes room for. It is radically disarmed of anything that could destroy the other who is essential to such a peace that bears fire within it. Such is its power to rule over all that there is no obstacle that cannot be moved aside. The image of moving a mountain—and it *is* an image, for which a literal meaning would be no less pathological than assuming that Jesus uses a sword of iron to break a household up (logion 16)—may then be taken here to refer to the otherwise unassailable and unmovable mountain of social convention and religious tradition.

> *49. Jesus said, "Blessed are the solitary and the chosen, because you will find the kingdom. For you have come from it and you will go there again."*

If one knows oneself as from the vine of the father, one *always* has access to the kingdom without going through the motion of observances or climbing the mountain of tradition, or entrusting oneself to an elite cast who presume to hold the keys of knowledge. Although only Thomas has been named among the disciples as a true solitary, the use of the plural form indicates that he is not the only one. At the same time, to be chosen and yet solitary stands in clear contradiction to the traditional notion of a "chosen race." The idea of election is extradited from the tradition in order to redefine it, as we saw already in logion 23. Seen in the context of everything that has gone before, there can be no question of a mandate here to forsake home and marriage in order to find the kingdom.

Nor can it mean to distinguish solitaries who have been chosen from those who have not, or vice versa. The solitary are the only elect, and the only elect are the solitaries. Those who have found the kingdom are those who discover where they have come from and where they are going—that place of life that lies right before their face. As Jesus says, the only difference from you who are listening to my words and those who have been chosen is that they have stand as persons who know themselves, as solitaries.

> *50. Jesus said, "If they say to you, 'Where did you come from?'*
> *say to them, 'We have come from the light, from the place*
> *where the light came into being by itself, established itself,*
> *and reveals itself in their image.' If they say to you, 'Is it*
> *you?' say to them, 'We are its children and we are the chosen of the living father.' And if they ask you, 'What is the*
> *sign of your father in you?' say to them, 'It is movement*
> *and rest.'"*

Jesus has just told us where we come from and where we are going: the kingdom. Here he offers a new answer: from the light. The words he uses are more obscure than any he has used so far, almost as if they were intended *not* to be understood. In fact, it is precisely the opposite. Given that "they" refers to those skeptical of what departs from conventional knowledge (logia 30 and 40), the answer is not intended to provoke a confrontation but to provoke a further request for clarification. Here we have a condensation of the method of the *Gospel* itself, namely, a secret (difficult to understand) saying that exposes the misunderstanding of the reader and stimulates the desire to understand. Although directed at outsiders, the effect is also to show the disciples, somewhat obliquely, what is expected of them as listeners to the words of Jesus.

Three aspects are singled out to explain what it means to come from the light: birth, grounding, and manifestation. The place where the light is born is at the same time the place of the unborn. That is, since the light came into being by itself, it was never born at all, or—which is to say the same thing—it is eternally coming into being. Thus to come from such a place means not to have left it behind but to be in touch with that which accompanies all our comings and goings, everything we have done and everything that is done to us, every word that is heard and every word that is spoken. The place where the light is grounded, as we have been told repeatedly in the *Gospel*, is self-knowledge. It is there that we are firmly rooted in the vine of the unborn father that nothing can uproot us. Without that knowledge not only are we easily uprooted (logion 40), but the light fails to illumine the kingdom that is all around us. That is, it fails to appear in the image that "they" and "we" share as human beings.

(The use of quotation marks to distinguish indirect speech creates a problem with regard to the referent of the word *they*. The context makes it clear that it refers to those questioning the disciples: they have their original image in the place where the light itself was born.)

The choice of words in this saying is unusual and merits a closer look to make sense.

Light, of itself, is invisible. Light cannot see light, any more than fire can burn fire or water wash water. It can be seen only in that which is not entirely itself the light, in that which blocks the light and casts a shadow. As children of our mothers who live embodied in the world and can only perceive it with our bodily senses, we are at the same time children of the light who make it visible and then actually see it ourselves. The light needs us to appear. To find the light within means to expose the whole of the world to the light. In the terms used earlier, in seeking to know ourselves as we find the kingdom.

In logion 43, the disciples asked Jesus by what authority he says what he says. Here Jesus invites the disciples to say of themselves what they have heard him say of himself. For this reason, he instructs them that if they are asked whether it is *they* who are the image of the light, they should reply that they are its children, not its father. Their election as images of the light is a result of their recognition of what is theirs by nature, not in virtue of any special gift denied to others. Furthermore, if they are asked for proof that their father is the unborn light, they should reply that they are at once motion and rest. In other words, because they are both born and living and at the same time coming from the unborn, they know themselves as a motion-at-rest and a rest-in-motion. The various activities enjoined on the disciples in the *Gospel* (seeking, desiring, thirsting) are not so much methods to find the kingdom as they are an appearance of the kingdom in the world. In this simple coincidence of the opposites of motion and rest we come to understand the sense in which the kingdom is only the search for the kingdom. Just as the sabbath was seen not as a reward for one's own labors but a dimension of the everyday (logion 27), so the only rest we can know as human beings is the knowledge that we are in the fullest measure what we truly are when we are searching for what we are not. In this knowledge of ourselves, the kingdom has found us.

The coincidence of terminology between this logion and the previous one adds something important to our understanding of the kingdom. Not only is it to be searched and found everywhere, but it is somehow identical to the unborn light. This leaves us with unanswered questions. For one thing, we want to know if that kingdom can *ever* truly be found by

us who are no more than images of it. For another, we want to
know in what sense we are to return to the kingdom of light
from which we have come. We suspect that rest and standing
in the light (logion 11) represent a kind of return, but the connections are not explicitly drawn.

> *51. His disciples said to him, "When will the rest of the dead
> come about, and when will the new world come?"*
> *He said to them, "What you look for has come, but you
> do not know it."*

It comes as little surprise that they disciples fail to grasp
what Jesus has just told them, evidenced in their understanding rest as the repose of the dead, rather than as a proof that
they are standing in the place of life. Their interest is in their
own future and a new world of the future. The irony of the previous logion is revealed here in that the disciples were asked
there to speak words that they were almost certain not to
have understood. They are anxious to be *told* by another what
requires personal insight to be understood; they wish Jesus to
know them rather than that they try to know themselves. They
seem to get his critique of transience of this world—how could
they not?—but assume that it will be replaced by *another*
world more or less like this one, but with a *different and better*
set of conventions and observances to follow. For Jesus, there is
no rest of the dead and no new world other than the rest and
the renewal to be found in this life here and now.

> *52. His disciples said to him, "Twenty-four prophets have spo-
> ken in Israel and they all spoke in you."*
> *He said to them, "You have disregarded the living one
> who is before you and have begun to speak of the dead."*

The disciples stubbornly cling to their preoccupation with the future, this time asking about whether the present moment is the future the prophets foretold. The number twenty-four can refer equally to the number of prophets recognized in the Hebrew Bible plus John the Baptist and to the twenty-four books of the Jewish scripture. There is no reason to choose since the point of the logion is the same: to be alive means recognizing what the past can and what it cannot do. The respondent is equally unclear. It could be Jesus and it could be Thomas, but the purpose is the same: to deflect attention from the person of Jesus as an individual and hence from aligning him with the voice of tradition—as if he were number twenty-five. The focus is turned instead on the living one who is not the one born under the name of Jesus but the unborn in whose name Thomas and Jesus, the twins, speak. The *Gospel* refuses to follow up on the implication of the disciples' remark, that he is in some sense the recapitulation of all the prophets. Nowhere is it said that no one before Jesus has seen what he has seen, and therefore that he speaks with the authority of the entirety of the scriptural tradition. There is no authority—not even the authority of Jesus—that can accomplish for the disciples what they must accomplish for themselves, namely, recognizing themselves too as twins.

> *53. His disciples said to him, "Is circumcision beneficial or not?"*
>
> *He said to them, "If it were beneficial, fathers would beget their children circumcised from their mothers. Rather, the true circumcision in spirit has become completely profitable."*

The cynicism of Jesus' answer to the question about circumcision is too obvious to miss. (The irreverence is all the more pronounced when we recall that James the Just, whose leadership is acknowledged in logion 12, was adamant in insisting on male circumcision for members of his community.) Jesus has already dismissed rituals performed out of duty as harmful to the spirit. Here he demeans a ritual by disassociating the medical procedure from its inner meaning in order to proclaim that the body is good just as it is born and does not need to be mutilated in the name of any religious or ascetic purpose.

Given the symbolic importance of the rite as a sign of divine election, this unmitigated rejection of physical circumcision not only reiterates the objection against the idea of a chosen race (as we saw in logion 23), but it also implies a rejection of the privilege of being born male. Only then does Jesus return to the spiritual meaning of the rite, what he calls true circumcision of the spirit which redounds to the benefit of the entire person. Not only must the mark of true election be seen as something spiritual; it also entails a blessing on the body as it is born of its mother.

Read in the context of everything that has gone before, there is no question of singling out circumcision as potentially harmful or beneficial in a way that other rituals are not. Rather Jesus takes the question of the disciples as just one more example of the view he has been rejecting all along.

54. Jesus said, "Blessed are the poor, for yours is the kingdom of heaven."

For the first and only time in the *Gospel,* Jesus speaks of the kingdom of heaven. Far from contradicting his earlier insistence on disassociating his idea of the kingdom from a heavenly realm, he is expropriating the vocabulary of those who guide us toward such a realm in order to give it a new meaning all of his own. It is not that Jesus wishes to proclaim material poverty as a blessing, though one may assume that he does mean to counter any of the many conventional views surrounding the poor as somehow cursed. The only poverty deserving of condemnation is that of being ignorant of oneself (logion 3). At the same time, if there is a true poverty that, like the true circumcision of the spirit, is a benefit, it can only be a detachment from those things of the world that we count as our possessions when in fact it is we who are possessed by them (logion 41), since they obstruct our knowledge of ourselves and hence our vision of the kingdom that is all around us.

> *55. Jesus said, "Whoever who does not hate father and mother cannot be my disciple and whoever does not hate brothers and sisters and carry the cross as I do will not be worthy of me."*

Just as Jesus had first told his disciples not to bother with ritual practices and later condemned them as sinful and corrosive to the spirit, so here, earlier remarks about setting the members of a household against one another (logion 16) are revised here to counsel hatred of one's family. These are strong words and seem unnecessarily so. If the only point is to insist on the construction of new relationships that supersede family ties, there seems no reason to despise the members of one's family, or to be more precise, their relationship to us. We have, therefore, to look between the lines for another, deeper meaning.

On the one hand, we recognize in them the earlier counsel that it is not enough to leave one household of conventions behind only to reconstruct another on the same foundations. The house has to be ransacked of what is of value in order to construct new values (logion 21). On the other hand, the ties to home are more than mere convention; they are a matter of one's identity as an individual. In hating my mother and father, it is not their *person* that I despise but the *ties* that define me as their child.

To hate one's parents and siblings, however, is not the same as detached indifference to family ties. It implies the continued awareness of the relationship in terms of which one has known oneself from birth, for as long as one hates, one's actions are in some sense defined by the memory of what is hated. To leave one's home behind without another thought is one thing. To bear the cross of remembering what was left behind is to require that the decision be made again and again. Hatred is far more painful than forgetfulness, and also more productive because it lingers on until either it turns into resentment or is overcome and absorbed into a new relationship.

The fact that Jesus identifies this as his own cross gives an indication of just how agonizing that decision was and continues to be. Clearly he does not *resent* his family but neither has the pain of the broken ties subsided.

At first glance, to bear that cross as he does contravenes Jesus' own injunction against doing what one hates (logion 6), but there is an important difference. There it was a question of not fulfilling religious duties out of a sense of obligation. Here it is a matter of hating what one has loved. In other words, we are asked to hate doing what we hate to do but which must be done. Obviously the renunciation of one's family in order to re-identify oneself as a child of the unborn father is a burden that we would prefer not to bear. At the same time, the fact that we hate doing what we hate doing means that in some sense we love it; only it is a kind of love that is more of a cross than a joy. To think otherwise is to anesthetize our natural human feelings, which the *Gospel* at no point demands.

56. Jesus said, "Whoever has come to know the world has found a corpse; and whoever has found a corpse, the world is not worthy of that person."

The reference to a cadaver here indicates an awareness that there is something dead about the world that we normally think of as alive, but this does not mean that this is all there is to be said. If the dark side of the world does not deserve one who has come to recognize it for what it is, nevertheless the world remains the locus of the kingdom, and in that sense both deserves and needs such knowledge. What is dead was once alive, and in the same way that senses deadened by habit can be restored, so can the world become the place of life to those who see everything there is to be seen in it.

57. Jesus said, "The kingdom of the father is like a man who had good seed. His enemy came at night and sowed weeds among the good seed. The man did not let them pull up the weeds but said to them, 'Do not go to pull up the weeds lest you pull up the wheat along with them.' For on the day of the harvest the weeds will be visible and will be pulled up and burned."

Continuing where the former logion left off, if the place of the kingdom is in *this* world and not some other, then it is a chiaroscuro of lights and shadows. And if the kingdom becomes manifest in a subversion of accepted values and ways of seeing, the ruling opinion about what is good and what is evil has to be overcome, not postponed for some final, apocalyptic judgment.

We have already seen how the kingdom grows wild and frustrates the attempts of those who try to cultivate it. In the image we are given here, it is the world, and not the kingdom, that is not being compared to a field of good seed, and the enemy who has sown it with weeds is not the world but the kingdom. The cultivator makes the naïve mistake of thinking that the weeds will not do enough damage to matter, and that there will be time to uproot them later—as if he had no idea of what weeds are and how they slowly choke the life out of a crop if left to spread. Like the mustard plant (logion 20), they invade the order of things imperceptibly at first, but as they increase and grow stronger, they overturn the order completely. The last becomes the first and is no more easily uprooted than the vine planted in the father (logion 40).

58. Jesus said, "Blessed is the one who has suffered and found life."

Suffering, toil, labor, and searching of themselves are of no value unless life is found in them. As we have seen, the discovery of the place of life in the world requires renunciation that is as heavy a burden for the seeker as the cross is for the condemned. (Like planting seeds, tending flocks, and dragging the sea for fish, the image of the criminal made to carry a cross to the place of execution was a common enough image for Jesus to use it metaphorically. Aside from a slight touch of irony, there is no indication that this has any reference to the way he himself died.)

59. Jesus said, "Look for the living while you are alive, lest you die and then try to see him, and you will be unable to do so."

Again, as he had in logia 15 and 37, Jesus insists that the living one can be seen. Lest there be any doubt, he makes it clear that the seeing is to be done here and now, in one's embodied person, before the light of our eyes is dimmed and it is too late. Seeing is not for another life, a question on which Jesus remains silent, neither affirming nor denying it because it is irrelevant to what he has to say in this *Gospel*. As a result, there is no reference in the text to death as a way to a greater life. Death is simply the absence of the kingdom, the final darkness, and nothing more. What is more, by using the generic term "living one" rather than a specific reference to himself as the living Jesus (as the narrator of the *Gospel* does in the incipit), Jesus again deflects any idea of his own uniqueness.

> 60. *They saw a Samaritan trying to steal a lamb as he was going to Judea. He said to his disciples, "Why does he stalk the lamb?"*
>   *They said to him, "That he might kill it and eat it."*
>   *He said to them, "He will not eat it while it is alive but only after he has killed it and it has become a corpse."*
>   *They said, "Otherwise he could not."*
>   *He said to them, "You, too, seek a place for yourselves in rest, lest you become a corpse and get eaten."*

The final sentence of the logion is hardly the explanation of the allegory one would have expected. The image of a Samaritan, a race of separatists despised by the Judeans, carrying a lamb to Judea suggests a story about a ritual sacrifice that would have been considered sacrilegious to a pious Jew. But Jesus asks his listeners rather to think of themselves as lambs that can only be eaten if they are first killed, and hence to find a place of rest to avoid that fate.

If only what is dead can be eaten, then one must protect oneself from becoming a carcass, either by dulling the mind or the senses, lest they be assimilated into the order of the world without awakening to the kingdom.

Once again, the place of rest is not a refuge *from* the world, but a rootedness in the kingdom *within* the world that gives meaning to every movement of the spirit.

> *61. Jesus said, "Two will be resting on a couch; one will die and one will live."*
>
> *Salome said, "Who are you, sir, to come up on my couch and eat from my table?"*
>
> *Jesus said to her, "I am he who is from the undivided. I was given some of the things of my father."*
>
> *Salome replied, "I am your disciple."*
>
> *Jesus said, "Therefore, I say, if one is undivided, one will be filled with light; but if one is divided, one will be filled with darkness."*

The couch onto which Jesus has stepped as an uninvited stranger is not a nuptial bed, but a place to recline for a meal. It is from there that he turns to his companion at the table, a certain woman named Salome, and announces that one of them will die and one will live. She does not seem as perturbed by his oracular pronouncement as she is anxious to know who he is and by what right he has invited himself into her home. He tells her that they are equals since he comes in virtue of what he has received from his father. Only when she proclaims herself his disciple, apparently having understood or at least shown herself eager to understand what that equality can mean, does he clarify the meaning of his opening words. Two people, both very much alive and reclining at the same meal, can yet be as different from one another as death is from life—one of them whole and full of light, the other divided and full of darkness.

These words seem to stand in contradiction to what we have been told of the need for an inner tension of opposites in order to reintegrate ourselves and become solitary ones. The wholeness that is spoken of here, however, is a quality that makes us equal to one another—that is, his twins—rather than something that divides and isolates. Accordingly, any duality creative of an elite is incapable of becoming one and must be overcome.

> 62. *Jesus said, "I tell my mysteries to those who are worthy of my mysteries. Do not let your left hand know what your right hand is doing."*

Although it sounds as if Jesus had selected Salome out for a special mystery reserved to a select few, we already know that his mysteries are for all, that the fire he guards was not cast only on the elect but on the whole world. His words here confirm that he would not have set his lamp on a lamp stand for all to see if he did not consider everyone worthy of the light.

The sense here is that one has not to worry about whether or not one deserves to know the mysteries of which he speaks; he would not promise that everything hidden will be manifest if we were not. One has only to worry whether one is using one's ears to hear or not.

This is what distinguishes Jesus' mysteries from the Pharisees who seek to keep the secrets secret by guarding the supposed key to understanding (logion 39). Hence the concluding proverb about the two hands must be taken to mean the opposite of keeping the truth hidden from the prying eyes of the unworthy. All attempts to hide, obfuscate, darken, encode, and mystify in the left hand what is offered openly and scattered to the four winds like a handful of seeds with the right must be avoided.

63. Jesus said, "There was a rich man who had a great deal of money. He said, 'I will put my money to use so that I might sow and reap and plant and fill my warehouses with fruit, and thus be in need of nothing.' This was what he thought in his heart, but that very night he died. Whoever has ears, let them hear."

Cultivating and harvesting for the future makes good sense, but in the end it smacks of death. Only if one is aware that we are only "passers-by" can everything taste of life. One needs to listen to conventional wisdom with the other ear, to know that death will one day take us, and that the most important thing before that happens is to see what death cannot take away (logion 59) because it was never born to begin with.

64. Jesus said, "A man had visitors and when he had prepared a banquet for them, he sent his servant to invite the guests.

"The servant went to the first and said, 'My master invites you.'

"That person said, 'Some merchants owe me money. They will come to me this evening; I must go and give them my orders. Please excuse me from the dinner.'

"He went to another and said to that person, 'My master invited you.'

"That person said to the servant, 'I have just bought a house and have been called away for the day. I will not have time.'

"He went to another and said, 'My master invites you.'

"That person said to the servant, 'My friend is going to be married and I am to prepare the dinner. I will not be able to come. Please excuse me from the dinner.'

"He went to another; he said to that one, 'My master invites you.'

> "He said to him, 'I have bought a farm and am on my
> way to collect the rent. I will not be able to come. Please
> excuse me from the dinner.'
>
> "The servant returned and said to his master, 'Those
> whom you invited to the dinner have asked to be excused.'
>
> "The master said to his servant, 'Go out on the streets
> and bring back whomever you find so that they may dine.'
>
> "Buyers and merchants will not enter the places of my
> father."

The reason that buyers and merchants live outside the places of the father is that they deal in things that pass away. Anyone who makes plans only to see them frustrated knows how badly life does at adjusting to our expectations of it. The host in this story is deliberately made to look foolish in order to stress the point. He prepares a dinner for his guests, but only when all the preparations have been made does he extend the invitation to them. Their excuses make more sense than his request. But rather than recognize his folly, he simply invited other guests, anyone prepared to come, so that this plan will have a semblance of success. Like the merchant whose only concern is to dispose of what he has to sell, the host thinks only of himself. In this regard, he is no different from the man in logion 63 who made all his preparations but forgot to take into account his own mortality.

> 65. He said, "A good man had a vineyard. He leased it to some
> farmers so that they might work it and he might collect its
> produce from them. He sent his servant so that the farmers
> would give the servant the produce of the vineyard. They
> seized the servant, beat him, and almost killed him. The
> servant returned and told his master.
>
> "His master said, 'Perhaps he did not know them.' He
> sent another servant. The farmers beat that one as well.

*Then the master sent his son and said, 'Perhaps they will
respect my son.' Since the farmers knew he was the heir to
the vineyard, they seized him and killed him. Whoever
has ears, let them hear."*

Like the former examples, the foolish landlord we meet
here is too stubborn and bent on reaping a profit to understand the cost. After seeing one servant after the other beaten
by his tenants he sends his own son who ends up murdered.
His greed for the fruits of his labors ends up in the death of
something much more valuable than his crop.

*66. Jesus said, "Show me the stone that the builders rejected.
That is the cornerstone."*

Jesus makes a parable of a familiar saying from the Psalms
of David and applies it to the former logion. In the normal
process of erecting a building, the words would not make
any sense, since the cornerstone is the first to be chosen, not
something picked up from stones rejected as unsuitable for the
construction. Unlike the keystone, which is the last stone to
be placed and hence has to be adjusted to what is already built
in order to give stability to the arch, a cornerstone is set first
and is useless to the stability of the structure. Its function is to
set the direction of a building, and everything added afterward
must adjust to it.

The meaning is thus that Jesus obviously intends to build
something oriented differently from the structure imagined
by the builders who have already discarded the cornerstone he
prefers to use.

*67. Jesus said, "One who knows all things but is lacking in one-
self lacks everything."*

Jesus here reiterates the importance of self-knowledge mentioned in logion 3, adding that proper knowledge of the world depends on knowledge of oneself. In this way he identifies the cornerstone mentioned in the former logion.

> *68. Jesus said, "Blessed are you when they hate you and persecute you. But they will find no place where they have persecuted you."*

Here we see an indirect, negative reference to what it means to be known, another consequence of knowing oneself (logion 3). Neither the place of life nor the place of the father nor the place of rest is to be found in places where the seekers who attend to the words of Jesus are persecuted, any more than a prophet can be appreciated by those who *think* they know him. One cannot be known by one's persecutors and despisers. And this is reckoned a blessing since their ignorance is a confirmation of one's own knowledge.

> *69. Jesus said, "Blessed are those who have been persecuted in their hearts. They are those who have truly come to know the father. Blessed are those who are hungry so that the belly of the one who hungers may be filled."*

On the face of it, there is nothing blessed about being driven away and not listened to. If so, Jesus would have to consider himself fortunate indeed, rather than complain that no one wants his medicine because they know the doctor too well (logion 31). But as we have just seen in the former logion, the closer the persecution cuts to the bone—to one's very heart—the surer one is that one has touched the core of what is wrong with the world and lit a spark in its darkness. So, too, in the same measure that ritual fasting is endured because it presumably redounds to one's own merit (logion 14), going hungry so that someone else may have their fill enhances the spirit in a way that mere conformity to practice cannot. Here the positive, illuminating function of the fire that Jesus has cast on the world in his call for a reversal of values is made plain.

> *70. Jesus said, "If you bring forth what is within you, what you have will save you. If you do not have that within you, what you do have within you will kill you."*

As we have just seen, even if the light that flows out of inner knowledge provokes persecution by those who remain in the dark, it is one's salvation. Salvation is not *brought about* by an outside, otherworldly force. What saves me is already within me, dormant, and needs only awakening to be brought forth. To do so, one must first know what is within: not just the memories of the past and aspirations for the future that accompany us on this side of death, but the vision of the living yet unborn father that does not taste death. Absent that vision, what would otherwise be our bond with life is said here to kill us. Obviously, ignorance does not bring about death in the ordinary sense, which will come to all of us eventually, quite apart from what we have known or not known. What dies is the capacity to know ourselves, smothered by illusions of knowledge that only deepen the darkness around the truth about ourselves, the world, and the kingdom that is within each of us if we would only seek it.

> *71. Jesus said, "I will destroy this house and no one will be able to build it."*

Unlike the house that Jesus plans to build with a new and rejected cornerstone, what he announces here he will destroy is the house of ignorance masquerading as the accumulated wisdom of convention and traditional values. In line with the progression from a milder criticism to a stronger one, here Jesus does not talk of sacking the house (logion 35) but of outright destroying it so completely that it cannot be rebuilt. There is more than hyperbole at work here. Insofar as the foundations of conventional thinking are illusory, it continues in existence only by virtue of the fact that it is believed in and inhabited. Once that belief has been made transparent, it collapses and there is nothing in our nature to assure that quite the same structure could ever come to be again. But the house of those who are homeless transients (logion 42) struggling to see what they can of the light while they are still alive (logion 59) cannot be destroyed because it has no walls to shut anyone out or protect anything within; indeed its custodians guard it against such construction, just as Jesus guards the fire and the bubbling spring (logia 10 and 13).

72. *A man said to him, "Tell my brothers to divide my father's possessions with me."*
He said to him, "O man, who has made me a divider?"
He turned to his disciples and said, "I am not a divider, am I?"

Jesus is astonished once again by the dogged insistence of his listeners on setting him up as an authority and reducing his words to the modes of thought in which they are most comfortable. Here his words about dividing a household (logion 16) and about the salvation that comes to those who are persecuted occasion the request that he stand in judgment on an inheritance dispute. Obviously the speaker has misunderstood completely and sees Jesus as if he were the harvester separating the weeds from the wheat. Not that the question does not deserve attention. But for Jesus to enter into the dispute would only risk further deepening the misunderstanding of what he is trying to say. The question with which he replies is ironic in that what is rhetorical for him is not so for his disciples.

> *73. Jesus said, "The harvest is great but the workers are few. So beseech the master to send workers to harvest."*

These words are a paraphrase, in declarative form, of the question Jesus had posed earlier about what is to be done by those who stand in the light (logion 11). They are a lament, the first in a series of three, that everything is ready at hand and yet no one is willing to make the effort to do what needs to be done.

> *74. He said, "Lord, there are many standing around the drinking trough, but there is nothing in the cistern."*

The unnamed someone in this saying could only be a twin of Jesus, perhaps Thomas himself, since it was he who we were told had already drunk of the bubbling spring that Jesus stands watch over (logion 13). Having learned his lesson, the title with which he addresses Jesus is not Master but the simple polite form of address, Lord, which Jesus does not reject. As he had done earlier, Thomas chides the disciples for their false expectations, this time by implying that they stand with the multitude gathered around an empty well.

> *75. Jesus said, "Many are standing at the door, but it is the solitary who will enter the bridal chamber."*

In the third and final lament, it is Jesus who speaks, confirming what had just been said with another image. Here we see again the apparent election of a few among the many who wish to pass through the door. But the only elitism is an elitism *in fact*, not *in principle*. There is no gatekeeper and no key. One passes through or one does not, but there is no demand to do so. We already know enough about the meaning of the solitary not to identify it with a secret knowledge, but here the idea of becoming one is given the sexual imagery of the nuptial chamber. The solitaries are "in place" there in virtue of an awareness of their dual identity (I am who I am because I am also what is not I) and the achievement of a unity that is a motion-at-rest and a rest-in-motion. The individuals who stand at the door without passing through may be isolated but never solitary.

> 76. Jesus said, "*The kingdom of the father is like a merchant who had a supply of goods and discovered a pearl. The merchant was prudent. He sold the goods and bought the pearl alone for himself. You, too, must seek his treasure that does not perish, where no moth comes to devour and no worm destroys.*"

The short simile explaining the kingdom of the father recalls the earlier simile explaining the nature of a human being (logion 8). In both the treasure is found not as a result of their search but only as a result of their capacity to *recognize* it when they saw it. Like the prudent fisherman who threw his entire catch overboard save the one great fish, the wise merchant in this tale disposes of all his possessions in order to retain what he has found, or more precisely, what has found him. To listen to these words, keeping in mind the mandate to keep searching, can only heighten our sense of not knowing what it is we are supposed to be searching for.

We have yet to be told in any concrete terms what that kingdom is. The cumulative effect of this and all the parables of the *Gospel* can only be the suspicion that, as far as we are concerned, perhaps the kingdom is only the eternal search for the kingdom. The pearl, the great fish, the place of life—perhaps they are not any*thing* or any*where*, but only that which we find out about ourselves in the process of looking for the one absolute that nothing on earth can eat away or corrupt. This is corroborated by the inconsistency in the story: Why should the merchant have to buy what he already has in his possession? Why look for that which is right in front of our face? Because, as we hinted at earlier in logion 3, the model of seeking-and-finding in the sense of effort rewarded needs to be replaced by one in which we seek for what we have already found.

> *77. Jesus said, "I am the light that is above all things. I am all: all things came forth from me and all things have reached me. Split a piece of wood; I am there. Lift up the stone and you will find me there."*

The Jesus who speaks here uses a different voice from the one we have been accustomed to. Always careful to deflect the attention away from his person and to renounce any title of or claim to authority, without any notice of what he is about, Jesus becomes the instrument of the light within him. The only explanation in the context of the *Gospel* is that the "I" who speaks these words is the living father who both is and is not the living Jesus. It is not the embodied Jesus who stands in the midst of the world as a manifestation of the unborn, but the unborn itself that manifests itself in the first person.

We saw a hint of this in logion 28, but the identification of the unborn with the kingdom that is everywhere, within us and without, that from which we have come and to which we are going (logion 50), can only be made *after* it has been made clear that this is not something unique to the person of Jesus, as we have already seen from the reference to the light within a person of light in logion 24, that is, only after we have learned that we are not disciples and Master, but twins.

We have already seen in logia 13 and 19 an image of the stones that carry within them the fire of the kingdom. Here, however, the reference to wood and stones is not merely metaphorical but both literal and metaphorical at the same time. It is as if we were being invited to split a wooden idol or turn over a stone statue, to see through *any image* or *any words* we have of the invisible light that we seek—including the "I" who speaks these words—in order to recognize it as a manifestation of the same light we bear within ourselves and that is visible only to those who have the wisdom to recognize it in the shadows it casts on the things of life.

> *78. Jesus said, "Why have you come out to the countryside? To see a reed shaken by the wind? And to see a man clothed in soft clothes like your kings and your great ones? They are dressed in soft clothes, and they are unable to understand the truth."*

The words of Jesus spoken here, as in logion 14, make it clear that he is talking to people who have left the city for the outlying districts or at least frequent those regions. There is a slightly sarcastic tone to his question that makes it rhetorical rather than a request for information. It is not a reaction to any particular comment of his listeners, but a general chiding for their failure to take advantage of the opportunity that is being given them. Instead of looking at the world they left from a new standpoint, they continue to see only what they *expect* to see, and to carry the whole weight of tradition and custom on their backs when it serves them nothing in the way of understanding Jesus' words other than occluding their vision.

> 79. *A woman in the crowd said to him, "Blessed are the womb*
> *that bore you and the breasts that nourished you."*
>
> *He said to her, "Blessed are those who have heard the*
> *word of the father and have truly kept it. For there come*
> *days when you will say, 'Blessed are the womb that has not*
> *conceived and the breasts that have not given milk.'"*

In yet another attempt to deflect attention from himself, Jesus inverts the words of praise addressed to him into a criticism. In expressing admiration of Jesus' mother for having given birth to such a son as he, the woman who speaks in this logion has seen only part of who he is. Jesus parries the adulation by implying that she has only seen what is born of woman and failed to listen to the words of the unborn father that were not nurtured in any womb or at any breast. When the time comes to rely on something other than our everyday existence, it is that which neither gives birth nor nourishes that merits real admiration. Jesus invites the woman to think of herself in larger terms rather than as one who conceives and gives milk, to replace the envy for his mother with the knowledge of the unborn that they both share with Jesus as children of that which lives without being born or raised.

> 80. *Jesus said, "Whoever has come to know the world has*
> *found the body, and whoever has found the body, the*
> *world is not worthy of that person."*

This needs to be read as a complement to logion 56 where the world was rejected as a corpse. Here the world, and with it the body, are recognized as possessed of a value that the dead world is not worthy of. The world is not dead except to those who do not recognize it as the place of life and of the kingdom, as Jesus has insisted from the start.

There is nothing esoteric about this discovery, nothing that requires initiation or special education to see. The only ones who do not deserve to see the world and the body anew are those impoverished by deliberate ignorance of themselves (logion 3).

> *81. Jesus said, "Let him who has become rich be king, and let him who possesses power renounce it."*

The enrichment of knowing oneself that comes to one who seeks and opens one's eyes to the kingdom was described at the outset as giving one the capacity to rule over all (logion 2). Although it was clear at the time that this rule did not entail subjecting everything to oneself as sole regent, we are told here that it does bring with itself a certain power that one did not have previously, as any increase of knowledge is bound to do. Lest that power subvert the nature of the kingdom, we are told here to renounce it for powerlessness, leaving us to conclude that any world over which we exercise power or authority has become a corpse and hence no longer the place of life.

> *82. Jesus said, "Whoever is near me is near the fire, and whoever is far from me is far from the kingdom."*

Renunciation of power for oneself does not mean handing it over to another. The fire that Jesus has cast on the earth and over which he stands watch can only be fanned into flame by those who stand close to where Jesus stands, that is, those who have knowledge of themselves as his twins. Those who think of him as a distant authority or power by that very fact distance themselves from the reign of powerlessness that he is urging us to seek.

83. Jesus said, "Images are visible to people, but the light within them is hidden in the image of the light of the father. He will reveal himself, but his image is hidden by his light."

With this logion we reach a turning point in the *Gospel.* Much of what seemed to be an unnecessarily radical over-turning of established ways of thinking will become a matter of course as the fundamental standpoint of Jesus begins to unfold. If his words have troubled before, the amazement that follows on that disturbance is about to overcome us in a way we could not have expected.

Despite the many references so far to seeing the light, the kingdom, and the father, there has always been a certain vague-ness about just how much there is to be seen. At times the *Gospel* speaks as if a reality hidden to the ordinary mind and senses makes itself manifest to those disposed to see it, but at the same time indicates that there is only an indirect disclosure by way of images. This was the case with logion 50, where the question is first taken up directly. At the time, we noted how light does not illumine light, that it can only be seen in con-trast to that which is not light. In that sense, pure light is as invisible as pure darkness. With that in mind, this tightly knot-ted saying is easily loosened and its important, though some-what unsettling, answer to the problem of what can be seen is made comprehensible.

An image, by its nature, is a reflection of something else. An image of the light refracts the light into shadows that enable us to see, if only indirectly, what is in itself invisible. Our inner nature—call it soul, knowledge, heart, the other ear, desire—is like a kind of light in the sense that it cannot be seen or understood except by its outer manifestation in the chiar-oscuro of the bodily senses. Seeing these manifestations not only as perceptions of the world but as refractions of an inner light enriches our knowledge of the world and of ourselves. They become, as it were, the disclosure of a kingdom that so permeates everything within and without that, like the light, it remains hidden without being sought in the play of light and darkness. The inner and the outer define one another and in so doing define the basic duality of our own human being.

What the *Gospel* adds to this idea of an inner nature hidden to us except through outer images is the idea of a greater, all-encompassing light. It is as if the interiority that we struggle to make visible by imagining it in terms of the outer world we can see were no more than a small ray of light generated by a greater source. It is not, therefore, just that the light within us is hidden from itself by reason of light being incapable of illuminating itself, but that even the little light we *can* refract through the images is immediately swallowed up by the light that no image can refract. And that very swallowing up *is* the manifestation of the light.

Lest we get too tangled up in the paradox of a smaller light disclosing itself by refracting itself in a greater light, the logion draws us back into the text by referring to this latter as the father's light, thus opening the way for us to paraphrase everything in terms of what is said elsewhere in the *Gospel*. The unborn that we bear within us is beyond our understanding, and yet if we do not acknowledge it, we are no more than our mother's children, born only one day to die like everything else in the world. The only proof we have of being children of an unborn father is the desire for something that death cannot touch (logion 76). To search for that which is undying because it was unborn is the only proof that we *can* search for it. And to know that much about ourselves is all there is to be found. Finding that we are born to search for something we cannot hope to find, restlessly in motion for a resting place that it is not ours to have—this is the mystery of our nature.

At the same time as this knowledge divides us against ourselves, it unites us as a family of those who have awakened to the mystery, and are therefore incapable of being satisfied with anything we can construct in the world to hide ourselves from this truth. It is like standing in the light and no longer being able to see anything, and then turning around to see what the light illumines, all the while remembering that the fullness of the light is at our back. Everything we see and everything we understand becomes a reflection, a mere image, and yet in that very act of watching all things become transparent, we recognize ourselves as an image of what is going on: the light seeking its own illumination, the unborn seeking life through those who are born and die. This is the kingdom of which Jesus speaks, the self-knowledge that rules over all by renouncing any illusion of the power to see through the light itself. Our father is disclosed as that which is forever hidden to us.

84. Jesus said, "When you see your likeness, you rejoice. But when you see your images that came into being before you, that neither die nor become manifest, how much you will bear!"

We are slowly coming to see what we have suspected from the start: there is an almost unbearable darkness hidden within the light of which Jesus speaks. As if to remove any doubt, to take away the little that we have left (logion 41), he now tells us in so many words that all our images of the unborn that we bear within us—of that which came to be before we did—can neither be ignored nor understood. Every intimation of the light is hidden by the light itself, and every attempt to dispose of those intimations is in vain. Every piece of wood we split,

every rock we lift reminds us of the fact that the only difference between darkness and light is that the light can know the
unknowable darkness within itself. As human beings, our only
escape from ignorance is knowledge of our ignorance. It is not
that part of us, the unborn, can be expected to survive while
another part of us will die.

Insofar as salvation has been defined as becoming one, the
idea of salvation by disintegration is foreign to the *Gospel*. Sim-
ilarly, were Jesus to speak of the unborn father as a kind of self-
knowing light in which we might, therefore, expect to share,
the picture would change radically. But he has yet to speak in
these terms, or even to give us any cause to believe in such a possibility. On the contrary, he contrasts the happiness that thinking in likenesses, similes, and parables bring with the great burden that comes from insight into the images of the light from
which we have come and to which we are going (logion 50)—
images that cannot make manifest what they mean and yet
refuse to die away. The earlier advice about putting an image in
place of an image (logion 22) ends up not delivering the joy of
release from conventional thinking but the awesome weight of
knowing the truth about who we are. In this way an answer to
the connection between rest, standing in the light, and returning to the kingdom of light is suggested: It is not that we live
in images while we are in the world and return to pure light
on leaving the world, but that we live completely enveloped
by the kingdom of light *in this life*. Becoming one entails both
finding the kingdom manifest in the movement of light and
shadow that characterize our activities in the world and turning our back on the world and its images to find repose in the
pure light of the kingdom where our individuality is no longer
visible. Our salvation as solitaries consists in seeing the things
of life *sub specie lucis* in this double sense.

85. Jesus said, "Adam came from great power and great wealth,
but he was not worthy of you. For, if he had been worthy,
he would not have tasted death."

Adam is presented here (as in logion 15) not as an image of
a paradise lost to which we will one day return but as an image
of that which we must surpass as not worthy of us, not only in
the sense that he is among the dead, as are the prophets of the
past (logion 52), but that he did not *return* to the great power
and wealth from which he was born. Adam seems to be an
image of a darkened and unintegrated mind. As sons of Adam,
we, too, are born ignorant but worthy of our origins; unlike
him, we need to fulfill the dignity of our origins by becoming
one and not tasting death.

86. Jesus said, "Foxes have holes and birds have nests, but the
child of humanity has no place to lay his head and rest."

The son of humankind is a general reference to every
mother's child who, unlike the animals, is born to be homeless.
Not even the discovery of the kingdom can give us refuge from
our human condition. To be, with Jesus, twins of the unborn
father means that our only repose is in movement, in being
passers-by (logion 42).

87. Jesus said, "Wretched is the body that depends on a body,
and wretched the soul that depends on these two."

To understand oneself only as a particular somebody born
of a particular mother is to have a miserable knowledge of oneself, to define ourselves only in terms of part of who we are. To
find repose in this for the restless, homeless searching of the
soul in so incomplete a self-understanding only increases the
impoverishment. One could say the same of the soul that seeks

repose in its unborn nature, ignoring the bodily relationship to the world. The body needs to be enriched by the soul, and the soul by the body, for us to become one with who and what we are. For either to depend on the other is a form of attachment that impedes the search for an integration of the two.

> *88. Jesus said, "Angels and prophets will come to you and give you what belongs to you. You, in turn, give to them what you have in your hands, and say to yourselves, 'When will they come and take what is theirs?'"*

What messengers and prophets have to give us is what is not theirs to give—or Jesus', for that matter—but is already ours, namely, awareness of the unborn father that is a part of our nature. By recognizing that same awareness in them, we are giving them what we have. In that awareness, that self-knowledge, the distinction between giver and receiver becomes irrelevant. The question we need to ask ourselves, therefore, is not who is to be great among us (logion 12), but how to rediscover authority, past and present, in terms of the appropriation of what belongs now, as it has always belonged, to the children of humankind.

> *89. Jesus said, "Why do you wash the outside of the cup? Do you not understand that the one who made the inside is also the one who made the outside?"*

The image of washing the cup reiterates what has been said about scrupulously observing rituals on the outside without taking into consideration our inner attitude, but seems to have been placed here for another purpose. The more immediate association we make from logion 87 is that just as the outside of the cup cannot exist without the inside, the notions of body and soul only have meaning as parts of an integrated whole.

While this is consistent with what has been said earlier about the mutual definition of flesh and spirit (logion 29), the problem is that we are told here that the same one who made the inside made the outside. So far there has been no talk in the *Gospel* of any "creator" of body and soul. On the contrary, we have been led to think of ourselves as containing within us something uncreated (logion 15).

> *90. Jesus said, "Come to me, for my yoke is easy and my lord-ship is gentle, and you will find rest for yourselves."*

We have already heard Jesus say that to approach him is to draw near to the fire (logion 82), to the passion to seek, to put to the torch our old ways of thinking, and illumine the darkness of our ignorance. Here it is a different voice that speaks, the voice of the unborn father who promises repose, a loosening of the yoke, and an undemanding rule. Yoke here refers to discipline or discipleship as a binding of two things together. Together they represent the movement-in-repose that is implied in being Jesus' twin.

> *91. They said to him, "Tell us who you are so that we may believe in you."*
>
> *He said to them, "You examine the face of the heavens and the earth, and yet you have not recognized the one who stands before you, nor do you know how to examine this moment."*

Having heard, but clearly not understood, the critical words about ritual washing and the promise of a light yoke, the disciples seem attracted by the relaxed asceticism and ask Jesus to identify himself so they can follow him as believers.

After having had their own views of who he is rejected (logion 13), they ask him to supply the proper title by which he wishes to be known. His reply plays on the hypocrisy of those who clean the outside of the cup and ignore the inside by telling the disciples they know how to sound out the external world around them and yet have no idea how to probe the present moment to recognize his presence before them. Yet again, he makes it clear that he has no intention of becoming an object of their belief, that he will not reveal anything that they cannot discover for themselves by sounding out what is right in front of their face.

> *92. Jesus said, "Seek and you will find. Those things you asked me about in the past, I did not tell you then. Now I am willing to tell you, but you do not seek them."*

These words follow immediately on the former. The repetition of the first words spoken by Jesus in the *Gospel*, the injunction to seek and find, have a richer meaning now than they did when first we heard them. Jesus seems to have expected this inasmuch as he indicates here that he has withheld saying certain things until the right moment. Now that enough has been said and he is ready to speak, he is prohibited from doing so because no one asks about them.

The reasoning seems odd, given that hardly anything he has had to say so far has been in response to the questions he has been asked, and we hardly expect him to turn around and start taking their earlier questions seriously. We can only assume that at some earlier point, before the time frame of the *Gospel*, his disciples put to him the kinds of questions he wanted but for some reason hesitated to answer, similar to what we saw in the case of Thomas in logion 13, who refused to answer a question that he was sure would be misunderstood. In any case, he begs his disciples to ask because he cannot ask for them, nor can he answer what he has now been asked.

---

93. "Do not give what is holy to the dogs, or they will throw them on the dung heap. Do not throw pearls to swine, or they might [...].

If the cynical proverbs Jesus repeats here are read as a continuation of the previous logion, as an expression of disappointment at how his words are wasted on the disciples, they would be completely out of character. Dogs and pigs were considered unclean animals and the Judeans would show their revulsion for non-Jews by referring to them in such terms, but the Jesus of this *Gospel* would hardly adopt such language toward his disciples, or even to refer to the mule-headed Judeans who cannot decide whether they hate the tree or the fruit more (logion 43).

Having seen Jesus' dislike for all forms of exclusivism and elitism, we need to read the words rather as an ironical repetition of that very criticism leveled at him for taking on such ordinary, ignorant disciples and encouraging them to ignore established religious authority. Here, as elsewhere, the oracular nature of the sayings often requires that we look for the meaning beneath the surface of what is actually said.

---

94. Jesus said, "One who searches will find, and one who knocks will be let in."

In contrast to religious leaders who hide the keys to knowledge and refuse to share with those they do not deem worthy, as if throwing pearls to dogs and swine, Jesus' only request is that his listeners seek and call out their questions. Once again, his choice of words is important. He does not say that we will find what we set out to find, only that whoever seeks will find—and probably something that will upset us before it amazes us (logion 2).

95. Jesus said, "If you have money, do not lend it at interest, but give to those from whom you will not get it back."

Just as fasting was vilified and going hungry so that others can eat was praised (logion 69), here giving money to those in need without expecting anything in return is presented as superior to giving with the ulterior motive of taking advantage of the recipient, whether in order to earn interest or to earn the merit of an almsgiver.

96. Jesus said, "The kingdom of the father is like a woman. She took a bit of leaven, hid it in dough, and made it into large loaves. Whoever has ears, let them hear."

In the ordinary course of life, one hides things so that others will *not* know about them. But it is the kingdom that is being talked about, and therefore we come to expect a reversal of the ordinary. Here what is hidden has the opposite effect of making its presence even more obvious than it would have been if shown and never hidden—like a spoonful of leaven in a lump of dough.

If the sayings of Jesus are secret, it is because they have taken on the nature of their subject matter and are best disclosed for all to see by being given time to work inconspicuously. The fact that leaven was considered in some sense unclean and hence forbidden in the house during the time of sacred feasts only reconfirms the fact that the way the kingdom works has nothing to do with religious observances.

97. Jesus said, "The kingdom of the father is like a woman carrying a jar full of meal. While she was walking along a distant road, the handle of the jar broke and the meal spilled out behind her onto the road. She did not know it; she did not notice any problem. When she arrived at her house, she put the jar down and found it empty."

As in the former logion, it is the image of a woman that is drawn on to speak of the kingdom of the father. There is no judgment passed on her failure to notice the gradual loss of her jar of meal, not even the implication that she should have been more attentive. Because of that, we are led to think of the kingdom as something that has to do with a gradual emptying of ourselves of the things that ordinarily sustain us. The image of a woman walking along the road with a heavy jar that gradually becomes lighter suggests that letting go of the values and ideas we carry around with us is not a matter of willful asceticism or deliberate planning, but something that happens as a consequence of our ceasing to give a thought to them. Like the farmer sowing his seed carelessly (logion 9), the changes that manifest the kingdom seem to take place not as a result of our efforts but by a letting go of effort.

98. Jesus said, "The kingdom of the father is like a person who wanted to kill a powerful man. He drew his sword in his own house and thrust it into the wall to see if his hand would carry through. Then he killed the powerful one."

For the first time in the *Gospel* the kingdom comes face to face with what seems a fundamental moral law and shows itself to be indifferent to ordinary morality. No mention is made of a justifying motive or attenuating circumstances. Someone plans the murder of a great person, that is all, and succeeds not *because* of his plan but quite by chance, once again like the spectacular crop that resulted from the careless scattering of seeds.

If this is what the kingdom is like, then it is not only prior to conventional mores and religious laws but in some sense also to human morality itself. If the kingdom belonged to a supernatural realm, one could seek justification for apparent immorality in a higher, divine will and providence. But if the kingdom is all around us and within us, and yet is not subject to human morality, then there is only one possibility remaining: the kingdom is identical with the natural order.

When we look back over everything Jesus has said up until now, the doubt about the relationship between the kingdom and ordinary morality has been flowing under the surface of the text all along, only now to emerge in dramatic yet clear form. We are driven to return and reread, looking for some indication that this is not the case, but there is nothing to inhibit, and indeed everything to sustain the translation of the notion of a kingdom in which those who let go of the world of conventional values fashioned in the human world are those who rule over all, into the notion of nature itself.

At the same time, just as social and religious conventions *as such* are not condemned or viewed as unnecessary, neither is the act of murder condoned in this logion. All that is said is that the kingdom is at work *everywhere,* whether we know it or like it or not. Only when that has been understood can one's trust in the unborn be complete; and only when that trust is complete can one seek to integrate the fact of being both a child of the unborn and a child of one's mother. And that awareness, by implication, is where moral values need to be rooted.

99. The disciples said to him, "Your brothers and your mother
are standing outside."
He said to them, "Those here who do the will of my
father, they are my brothers and mother. They are the ones
who will enter the kingdom of my father."

Note that the brothers and mother are standing outside.
Jesus—or he, the solitary and twin, it does not matter—wish
them inside, in a new relationship that answers to the will of
the father rather than to the will of social convention. This is
the first time in the *Gospel* that reference is made to the unborn
as having a will of its own. Were it not for the identification
of the kingdom of the faith with nature, this might suggest a
higher but invisible world of divine providence to which we
have ultimately to answer. But since we are the children of the
father, and since the kingdom of the father is not only within
us but all around us, the father's will belongs to our nature just
as our nature is enveloped in the larger natural order around
us. Everything that is to be known about the will of the unborn
is hidden, like a spoonful of leaven, in the recesses of the natural order. We cannot know ourselves without awakening to
that fact and becoming attentive to the manifestation of the
unborn light in the images of this transient world of ours.

100. They showed Jesus a gold coin and said to him, "Caesar's
men demand taxes from us."
He said to them, "Give Caesar's things to Caesar; give
God's things to God; and what is mine, give to me."

In response to a specific question about legal obligations,
Jesus presents an ascending order of values, the higher relativizing the lower, just as a smaller domain is located in a greater
kingdom. In giving to the god what belongs to the god, what

belongs to the emperor loses its absoluteness, like a smaller circle encompassed by a larger. And in giving to Jesus what is his, what is the god's is also deprived of its absoluteness and located within a wider sphere. This arrangement makes it clear that the kingdom of heaven, or the kingdom of the father, is wider and more inclusive than the kingdom of the gods. This is the only time in the *Gospel* that reference is made to a single deity. But, as in logion 30, Jesus neither affirms nor denies the idea of another world or anything in it. He simply sets the matter aside as if to say: Let the gods take care of the gods, one or many though they be. The important thing is to give Jesus what is his.

We already know from logion 88 that this giving is not a request to hand anything over of our own or to return something to its rightful owner. It means awareness of what already belongs to Jesus, quite apart from whether we recognize it or not. In other words, giving Jesus what is his means seeing him for who he is as distinct from who we might wish him to be. As we saw, the complement to knowing oneself is to be known, and Jesus simply asks to be known as he knows himself.

> *101. Jesus said, "Whoever does not hate his father and his mother as I do cannot be a disciple to me. And whoever does not love his father and his mother as I do cannot be a disciple to me. For my mother according to the flesh gave me death, but my true mother gave me life."*

This is the third time Jesus repeats his remark about breaking ordinary family ties in order to acknowledge a new realm of relationships. Read as a continuation of the previous logion, it is as if he is drawing another, still smaller circle within the kingdom of the emperor in order to dispossess it of any claim to absoluteness. At the same time, he tells us here what had only been implied in his earlier injunction to hate one's father and mother: this hate, if properly understood, makes possible a new way of loving them. It is a matter of conjecture how to complete the broken text of the final sentence, but even with the ellipsis in place, it seems clear that to love one's parents as Jesus does requires a distinction between the mother who bore us in her womb and the true source of one's life. This, too, would relativize our reference to the unborn light from which we have come as our father and allow us to speak of it as our mother as well, in effect making the male and the female one (logion 22). Recalling the metaphor we adopted in trying to unravel logion 83, it is as if I turned my back from the image of the father in which the source of life is refracted to face the blinding pure light in which there is no distinction, and then returned to the world of imagery to see that the father can just as well be called the mother.

> *102. Jesus said, "Woe to the Pharisees, for they are like a dog lying in the cattle manger; it does not eat, nor does it let the cattle eat."*

The metaphor of the dog in the manger was as well known to Jesus' listeners as it is to us from Aesop's fables. Consistent with Jesus' earlier criticism of the Pharisees as having hidden the keys of knowledge from others without even having bothered to seek that knowledge for themselves (logion 39), they are here likened to a dog who neither eats nor allows the oxen to eat what is in the manger. The message, once again, is to avoid deciding in terms of existing conventions who is worthy of the secret sayings and those who is not. Furthermore, by likening the Pharisees to dogs, he again turns their own prejudices against them (logion 93).

> *103. Jesus said, "Blessed is the man who knows where the rob-*
> *bers will enter, so that he will rise, gather his forces, and*
> *gird up his loins before they come in."*

Mention has already been made of the need to protect
one's inner house against the thieving intrusions of conventional thinking (logion 21). The suggestion made here is that
this will require not only that we have been able to recognize
that which truly belongs to us, but that we stand prepared
at all times. Jesus earlier referred to himself as the custodian
of the fire and of the bubbling spring. We are now made to
understand that his unrelenting criticism of those who would
expropriate it into ordinary, discriminating knowledge is his
way of girding his loins against the thieves. Ruling over all, in
this sense, is not the posture of complacency of one who has
conquered everything and found safe refuge, but a repose-in-
movement that must continually be on its guard.

> *104. They said to him, "Come, let us pray today and let us fast."*
> *Jesus said, "What sin have I committed? By what trans-*
> *gression have I been overcome? But after the bridegroom*
> *has left the bridal chamber, then let people fast and pray."*

As we have come to expect, the disciples completely mis-
understand the point of girding one's loins and assume that
they are to begin praying and fasting at once. The suggestion
is discarded sarcastically by reminding his listeners, in the
first place, that from where they stand, such things are acts of
repentance and as such assume that there is some sin to repent
of; and second, that if he were to renounce his earlier rejection
of such acts as sinful and harmful to the spirit (logion 14), this
would amount to a declaration of defeat in the face of their
religious conventions. Against these assumptions, Jesus makes

his own position clear: let those who have given up the search to become one return to their former ways of prayer and fasting. In other words, give to religion what belongs to religion but keep it away from those solitaries who have entered the nuptial chambers (logion 75).

105. Jesus said, "One who knows one's father and mother will be called the child of a whore."

We have already been told to hate father and mother as Jesus does—as a cross to be born (logion 55)—so as to love them the better (logion 101). Here we are warned that to know one's parents in this way is to call on one's head the curse of the whore's child, to be seen as one outside the bounds of the house of conventions, a homeless illegitimate. The rumors circulating about Jesus being the bastard son of Mary and a Roman solider must have come to the mind of his listeners, though the point of his remark is more general and refers to anyone who has discovered his true ancestry outside the normal family ties, in the unborn light of the father, in the true mother.

106. Jesus said, "When you make the two one, you will become children of humanity; and when you say, 'Mountain, move away,' it will move."

From the point of view of Jesus, those who are no more than whores' children to the eyes of the world are the true children of humanity. The solitaries who have entered the bridal chamber to make the two one (logia 22 and 105), those who have become integrated by making peace in their house among the two who dwell there, are not deterred by an apparently unmovable mountain of ordinary conventions (logion 48). They rule over all other kingdoms of the world.

*107. Jesus said, "The kingdom is like a shepherd who had a
hundred sheep. One of them, the largest, wandered off.
The shepherd left the ninety-nine and sought the one until
he found it. After his toil he said to the sheep, 'I love you
more than the ninety-nine.'"*

To the four previous analogies of the kingdom (logia 20, 57,
76, and 96), Jesus now adds two more. Here it is said to be like
a large sheep of greater value than the rest of the flock of one
hundred, much like the fisherman in logion 8 who dumped
the rest of his catch overboard once he had found the big fish.
The shepherd does not pay particular attention to the sheep
until it strays from the flock; it is only then that he must for-
get everything else and seek it out. In other words, as we have
seen in other of these logia, one needs to search for what one
has already found, or rather for what separates itself and chal-
lenges our habitual way of looking at things. To attempt to see
it within the flock would be like trying to stretch two bows at
the same time (logion 47).

*108. Jesus said, "Whoever drinks from my mouth will become
like me and I will become that person; and the things that
are hidden will be revealed to that person."*

Here we are presented the first indication that to know
oneself as Jesus' twin means not only that I become like Jesus
but that he becomes me. There is clearly more going on in the
image of drinking from the mouth of Jesus than a mere figure
of speech for receiving a revelation of hidden things. A transfer
of identities is taking place that transforms both the speaker of
the secret words and the one in whom they come to light. Like
two mirrors facing one another, anything that stands in the
light between them belongs to both and makes them belong

to one another so that giver and receiver, given and received, image and imaged become indistinguishable. The very structure of language distinguishing subject from object is broken down so that one's mouth is not capable of saying what it is like without being misunderstood (logion 13). Jesus the twin and Judas the twin become one, each knowing himself and being known by the other in a way that can be likened to no other relationship, not even that of parent and child.

> *109. Jesus said, "The kingdom is like a man who had a treasure hidden in his field but did not know it. When he died, he left it to his son. The son, not knowing of the treasure, took the field and sold it. The buyer went plowing and found the treasure. He began to lend money at interest to whomever he wished."*

In this last simile of the kingdom, Jesus implies a contrast between a treasure that is found by one who is seeking and the treasure that is found by one who is not. The former, we would suppose from what has been said already, would have the prudence and wisdom (logia 8 and 76) to hold on to what has been found and to continue seeking; the latter, depicted here, foolishly values it as a conventional treasure and does not hesitate to forfeit it for immediate profit. The one who finds is less fortunate for the finding, since not only has he not been searching but he ends up devaluing the need to search. It is the reverse of the Pharisees who hold the keys to the treasure but hide them; here one has stumbled on the treasure but has not the eyes to recognize it for what it is.

> *110. Jesus said, "Let whoever has found the world and become rich deny the world."*

Jesus brings the double meaning of the world together in the same sentence in order to reconfirm what was just said. The insight into the world—the *whole* world, that within us as well as that without us—is like a hidden kingdom suddenly come into the open before one's very face. All things are seen to be images refracting a pure, invisible light. Knowing what one has discovered means that one can never see things again with quite the same eyes. It means renouncing the world as it had been known in order to know the world for what it is. To put the same thing in other words, it means that anything that I can find in the world cannot itself be the truth of the world but only something to be *seen through*. The marvel of this insight, far from concluding the search, is that the end of the search is its beginning (logion 18), the finding is a renunciation of all finding understood as an end of seeking.

> *111. Jesus said, "The heavens and the earth will roll up in your presence, and whoever lives from the living one will not see death."*
>
> *Does not Jesus say, "The world is not worthy of one who has found himself"?*

Finding the world *as it is* and renouncing the world *as we thought it was* is like seeing the whole of the cosmos rolled up before one's very eyes like a scroll that has been opened up and read through to the end. Drinking from the mouth of the living Jesus is like looking at all things that come to be and pass away in this transient world, and seeing life where one had earlier seen only death. These are the words of Jesus, repeating the promise that had been made in logion 1 by Thomas. The comment that follows echoes the voice of the Twin, recalling the words Jesus had spoken regarding knowledge of oneself (logion 3) and knowledge of the world (logia 56 and 80).

112. Jesus said, "Woe to the flesh that depends on the soul; woe to the soul that depends on the flesh."

We have already heard Jesus express his admiration at how flesh and spirit manifest one another and arise from one another (logion 19). As with all other expression in the *Gospel* of the duality that marks our human condition, it is the integration of the two, not the conquest of one by the other, that constitutes true knowledge of oneself. The false dualism, in which either flesh or spirit lords it over the other as a mere dependent, is roundly condemned. The introduction of the same idea a second time in stronger language is something we have seen occur at several points through the *Gospel*. It not only serves to keep us in mind of what has been said or to reiterate it in stronger and more radical terms, but to indicate a specific context for sayings that were originally given as general statements. In this case, the effect is to remind us of the importance of balancing insight into the unborn, invisible, unspeakable place of life and light with a recuperation of the sensual, embodied nature that is ours as children of our worldly mothers.

113. His disciples said to him, "When will the kingdom come?" He said, "It will not come by expecting it to come. It will not be said, 'Look here' or 'Look there.' Rather, the kingdom of the father is spread out over the earth, and people do not see it."

The circle of sayings that was opened with the first three logia of the *Gospel* is closed now in almost the same language. The disciples are the same, men who do not see what has been scattered before them without any distinction as to rank or tribe or gender. They still ask after the future without having learned to see that, like the *Gospel* itself, the end was already in the beginning (logion 18). The difference is that the speaker who responds here is not identified as Jesus. There is no reason to do so. He is not a master on whose authority the sayings are to be believed; he is not possessed of a secret knowledge intended for an elite few. He never was. His person here becomes transparent, and his words are left to speak for themselves, as they were intended to be from the start. There is nothing hidden that has not been revealed (logia 5 and 6)—including the true source of the words that Jesus has spoken.

> *114. Simon Peter said to them, "Let Mary leave us, for women are not worthy of life."*
>
> *Jesus said, "Look, I will guide her to make her male, so that she, too, may become a living spirit resembling you males. For every woman who makes herself male will enter the kingdom of heaven."*

The *Gospel* does not conclude where we expect it to. In closing the circle of the sayings, we had arrived at a kind of movement-at-rest. The ending sets that rest in motion again, throwing us off balance in much the same way as we fall forward in order to take another step. The final dialogue, placed at the end as it is, receives special importance. It is not just that we are in a better position to understand what might have seemed slanderous if introduced out of context. The subject matter of the exchange with Simon Peter touches a nerve in the conventional wisdom that is as sensitive now as it was then: the equality of women in the natural order.

We have already seen two women disciples appear in the *Gospel*, Mary (logion 21) and Salome (logion 61), but nothing was said of their gender. The purification that circumcision accords the male in the traditional religion of the disciples was dismissed as prejudicial to the inherent goodness of the body as it was born (logion 53).

The impurity that cannot be lifted from women, and which, according to Simon Peter (whose unkindness to women was legendary), renders them unworthy of life, was not mentioned directly. But it was implicitly rejected again and again by redefining the unworthy as those who refuse to break ties with the conventions of the world (logia 55, 56, 62, 80, 85, and 111), as also by the injunction to make the male and the female into one (logion 22). Simon Peter seems to have understood that the implication and the doubt he voices represent the final dichotomy to be challenged by Jesus.

As usual, Jesus makes his point obliquely, only hinting at the consequences of what he says lest it be taken as a mere principle to be accepted on faith rather than an insight to be earned by interpreting the saying (logion 1). Unlike the keepers of tradition who misguide their followers (logion 3), he offers to guide women toward their maleness in order that they may find the place of life in the kingdom.

The transformation is clearly intended to enhance women and to liberate them, not to take away what is theirs. The duality between men and women needs to find a new integration that respects the mutual definition of flesh and spirit (logia 19 and 112). To paraphrase what was said of circumcision in logion 53, if women were inferior to men, they would have been born male. And just as the true circumcision is of the spirit, then the true maleness of the women lies in the spiritual integration of the male and the female.

The immediate conclusion for anyone who has ears to hear is that the same holds true of the male. The concluding words of the previous logion indicate that the kingdom cannot be sought here *or* there, but only here *and* there.

The Gospel According to Thomas

The title of these collected sayings of Jesus has a richer meaning placed at the end than it would have had at the beginning. It does not refer to the goodness of the messenger, a designation Jesus had rejected (logion 13), but to the goodness of the message. And the authority in whose name this message has been written down is not Didymos Judas Thomas, but only Thomas, the Twin of Jesus.

Saeculum

Placing the text

As CHILDREN of our times, we are not satisfied with reading a sacred text merely in the profane world of the academy or in the sacred precincts of the temple. In the end, our reading has to be exposed to the spirit of the age that surrounds them both and brings its own questions and doubts. The time has come, therefore, to step out of the *fanum* and into the *saeculum*. Just as scholarship is not an engagement with the text itself but only with the circumstances of its birth, so too, entering into the text as a kind of sacred space, even if set within the landscape of scholarship, does not address the problem of whether and to what extent the text is convivial—though not necessarily coincident—with our view of the world. It begins in a shift from a hermeneutic of dialogue to a hermeneutic of suspicion.

PLACING THE GOSPEL OF THOMAS

The overriding suspicion that we face on leaving the precincts of the *fanum* is the rupture with received tradition that the *Gospel of Thomas* effects. This was touched on briefly and in general terms in our review of the scholarly work that has been done on *Thomas*. The extent of the differences is much clearer now that we completed our reading. At the same time, it should be equally clear that since anything like an "objective" account of the sayings is impossible, the contrast with tradition is already colored by the lens through which we view the text.

In my commentary, I refrained from any attempt to sift out the "gnostic" Jesus from the "canonical" one. Both categories seemed to me prejudicial to the attempt to assume an internal unity to the text and to read it as far as possible on its own terms. On the other hand, I am only too aware that what I have read *out* of the text differs considerably from what scholars comparing it to literature of the same time and genre have been able to read *into* it. Our purposes are different. I have sacrificed all concern with the authenticity of its portrait of Jesus in order to focus on its archetypal qualities. The way in which a particular person at a particular time and place is seen to recapitulate the needs and expectations of a group of people, to fill up with new meaning symbols that have become hollowed out through indifference, doubt, or irrelevance, and to survive major transitions of social order and ways of thinking, remains one of the great mysteries of human history. The mystery only deepens when we find a figure, like the Jesus of the *Gospel of Thomas*, that has somehow retained its archetypal qualities after having disappeared for nearly sixteen hundred years. There is no need to jump to the conclusion that we have come in touch with timeless truths that transcend language, culture, and the progress of knowledge. It is enough to recognize that there is a certain diachronicity that allows us to feel challenged in its presence.

While I lack the confidence that the reading given in the previous pages is fair in all aspects, I feel there is an internal consistency of perspective that discloses itself through its play of double meanings, ambiguities of expression, and apparently disconnected strings of oracular-sounding sayings. This consistency does not emerge from the surface of the text; it requires an acceptance of the invitation to try and stand where Jesus stands when he says what he says. The purpose of the text as stated in its incipit is to keep alive, through interpretation, something that would otherwise smack of the dead and gone. The index of this rehearsal of Jesus' words is Thomas, the twin. The only evidence of its truth is that readers recognize this same twin in themselves.

To know the ancestry of a particular phrase is no guarantee that one has understood its meaning in this text. Admittedly, there are numerous cases of ellipsis and haplography in the manuscript that may still be reconstructed in new and enlightening ways and even alter the meaning of other parts of the text. My only point is that nothing scholars will come to unearth about the origins and composition of *Thomas* is likely to argue against the benefit of reading it as a unity with its own distinct point of view. True, its portrait of Jesus is more like a mosaic than the seamless robe that the canonical gospels try to weave. This does not require, however, that we postpone looking at the pattern of the whole until we have disassembled it to look at each piece, asking who made it and of what material. Of course, one is always free to rearrange the pieces into something more familiar and less conflicting with theological and scriptural tradition, and many have already attempted to do just this. For myself, I prefer to struggle with the fragmented mosaic such as it is.

Is *Thomas* then a new wineskin that would sour the aged wine of tradition? Is accepting it as scripture within established Christianity trying to draw two bows at once? The question cannot be answered directly in this simple form. We have first to decide *what* it is in the complex, multifaceted reality we call Christianity that it is being measured against.

To see it as a kind of "fifth gospel" assumes that the primary frame of reference is the four canonical gospels of the New Testament. Archaeologically speaking, this makes good sense, since it brings us back to the earliest strata of oral and written tradition that produce those books, and because it gives us a different view of what Jesus taught. Historically speaking, however, the comparison seems misguided. The canonical gospels can no longer be defined primarily as first-century documents. They have shaped, and been shaped, by an entire history of theological reflection and institutional development that has long since become their primary frame of reference. Their roots in tradition have come to determine the weight given to them as records of the actual life and teachings of Jesus. The place of the *Gospel of Thomas* in that tradition was decided with its banishment in the fourth century. Attempting to reverse that decision may have consequences for that tradition from now on, but it cannot change the past. For now, viewed as a "new gospel," *Thomas* can only speak as a voice from outside the tradition.

This in turn leads to a clean division of opinion about its value as a "sacred scripture." On the one hand, we see those who welcome *Thomas* with open arms as a relief from the entire Christian doctrinal heritage. We see this, for instance, in the surprisingly perceptive poetic paraphrase of the gospel by the mystical author Erik van Ruysbeek, whose initial reaction on reading the text was to discover in it a spiritual identification absent in the orthodox view of Jesus he had been raised with. In his words, "This Jesus could be my Jesus, its superiority leaving behind the ecclesiastical dogma of the religion of my youth."[1]

On the other hand, we see a noted historian of early Christianity like John Meier rejecting the idea of the "kingdom" presented in *Thomas* on the grounds that it does not concur with ecclesiastical tradition:

> The idea of the kingdom of God as a purely interior, invisible, present spiritual state of individual hearts is a foreign intrusion. It is at home in 2d-century Christian Gnosticism (so the *Gospel of Thomas*, sayings 3, 51, and 113), 19th-century German liberal Protestantism, and some 20th-century American quests for the historical Jesus, but not in the canonical Gospels in general or Luke in particular.[2]

What I mean to suggest there is that there are other ways to appropriate *Thomas* into Christianity than closing the door on it or trying to expand the New Testament canon to accommodate it. We have to take what we have in order for it to have meaning for us, not in order to conjecture meaning it *might* have had. In particular, I suggest that we see *Thomas* as a bridge to a multi-religious spirituality and to the recovery of the mystical tradition. To locate it within this genre is not only consistent with the interpretation presented in these pages but responsive to the demand for Christian self-understanding to interact with the spirit of the saeculum. In other words, extraditing *Thomas* from its definition as a heretical form of Christianity at the same time helps to extradite the Christian tradition itself from its self-imposed limits.

THE EXTRADITION OF THE THOMAS TRADITION

The dialogue among religions, which has been pursued with cautious but growing enthusiasm across the Christian world during the latter half of the last century, has found much wider acceptance among those seeking a "spirituality" receptive to the wealth of a plurality of traditions long at odds with one another. Straddling the established frameworks of doctrine and religious practice is no longer an esoteric, heretical imperative of malcontents. It has become a representative religious posture of the saeculum. Among world religions, this is most evident among those raised in predominantly Christian and Buddhist cultures, but as those cultural borders have bleared, so have the definitions of religious affiliation.

Unlike the flurry of new religious movements offering a supra-traditional synthesis, little clear leadership has emerged from within the established religions with enough sensitivity to the spiritual mood to offer an alternative way of "belonging" to one's own tradition while claiming as one's rightful inheritance what lies outside of it. What does exist, for example, in the way of Christian commentaries on Buddhist scriptures and Buddhist commentaries on Christian scriptures goes largely ignored by the leadership of both Buddhism and Christianity. In such a fluid and uncertain situation, a text like the *Gospel of Thomas* is more than a challenge to received Christianity. It offers a bridge between religions.

The extradition of the Jesus of the *Gospel of Thomas* from canonical norms and its relocation in the realm of contemporary spirituality as an interreligious bridge is not just a response to a current need. It is suggested by the text itself. The general religious and theological world within which Jesus' sayings were collected was probably every bit as open and pluralistic as our own. At the same time, as a Galilean Jew whose religious customs differed from those of the Judean Jews among whom he traveled, Jesus was aware of the resistance of orthodox leaders to whatever did not accord with their own ways of thinking. He found himself at home in the "desert" between the two worlds, and this in turn made it easy for those of his followers sympathetic to the extra-traditional religious life of the age to make him a mouthpiece for a new spirituality willing to trespass established boundaries.

In preparing my commentary on *Thomas*, I deliberately tried to remain within the vocabulary of the text in such a way that it would make sense to those with only a modicum of knowledge of Christianity's doctrinal history. The closer I looked at the sayings, the more aware I became that with no need to redefine any of the terms outside of their usage in the text, everything the Jesus of this gospel has to say is congruent with Buddhist teachings on the detached, awakened mind. This is remarkable, given that more than 80 percent of the text consists of words found more or less in the same form in the canonical gospels. Buddhism is, of course, a complex and richly varied body of doctrines, and not everything is compatible with everything else as one moves from country to country and age to age. What is more, if there is much in Buddhist doctrine—most notably, the ethic of selfless activity—that is barely touched on in Jesus' sayings, neither is there anything inconsistent with it. If one wishes to view the person of Jesus through spectacles composed of one Christian lens and one Buddhist, without everything becoming a dizzy blear, the *Gospel of Thomas* offers the bridge and the frame to hold them in place.

Although I do not discount the fact that I live and work in a predominantly Buddhist country as having affected the way I interpret *Thomas*, the more important consequence of this coincidence is that the text represents the clearest invitation we have among all the early texts of Christianity to a fully Buddhist reading of Jesus and his teachings. The overlaps between Buddhist awakening and *gnosis* to be found in other works of the Nag Hammadi library would soon enough be overshadowed by the sort of dualistic cosmology that Buddhism has consistently opposed throughout its long history. Not so with *Thomas* where the words of the living Jesus so closely resemble those of the Buddha, without any interference of doctrines that have long kept the two traditions apart, that there is certain to be much more beneath the surface for the keen eye of a practicing Buddhist to uncover. The kind of challenge the text presents to Christians, not to mention Jewish or Islamic believers, is more direct, in that its language is so often a clear affront to established ways of thinking. The Buddhist, in contrast, being at a greater distance from received thinking about Jesus, is likely to pass this over without a second thought, and hence to open a way for these two great spiritual streams to flow into one another.

In this sense, the *Gospel of Thomas* stimulates us to do something we have known for a long time we needed to do but which requires a spiritual discipline difficult in the extreme: to see Jesus through the eyes of the living Buddha and to see the Buddha through the eyes of the living Jesus—something only a twin can hope to achieve. The genius of the text is that it offers the follower of Buddha an uncommonly ready access to the teachings of Jesus at the same time as it opens the doors of Buddhist doctrine to the follower of Jesus.

No sooner is this said, however, than we are reminded of the suspicion that the *Gospel of Thomas* has broken so radically with Christological thought through the centuries, not to mention with the uncompromising monotheism it shares with Judaism and Islam, that in its encounter with Buddhist doctrine it cannot be said to represent the Abrahamic tradition, and that consequently any confluence would be self-defeating for Christianity. The key to overcoming the difficulty, perhaps the most serious obstacle to recognizing *Thomas* as a Christian text, lies in a posture of humility toward doctrine that the long political and intellectual struggles of Christianity have all but eclipsed.

The assumption that *Thomas'* Jesus means to dispose of any teachings except those that are mentioned in the sayings is patently false. It deliberately renounces their use, yes, but for a purpose. The gospel does not offer a complete system of beliefs and practices, but only a path for those who seek that place in human experience where such beliefs and practices are born— for as long as they seek it. Its critiques are all provisional and conditional on overcoming the conventional wisdom that the ground of faith lies in the authority of texts, venerable predecessors, or established customs. The only purpose of the text is insight into our own nature. It offers no principles of community organization, no ethical guidelines, no cosmology, and no theology. Its injunctions to homelessness, transience, the breaking of family ties, the renunciation of religious observances, and the relativizing of all external authority are not intended as a blueprint for living. All these things, as well as all the criticisms raised against them, are no more than what Buddhism calls *upāya* or "useful means" for seeing what there is to see.

To say that the truth of doctrine is provisional on insight it produces, that all religious beliefs are ultimately humbled by the higher end they point to but can never adequately express, leaves too many questions unanswered to form the foundations of a full tradition of faith and practice. At the same time, insofar as Christianity has to do with awakening from the darkness of ignorance about ourselves and seeing through the conventional way of thought that tether us so closely to the tradition that we can never reach its wellsprings in our own natures, then the sayings that Jesus spoke and Thomas wrote down belong to the life of Christianity—indeed to the life of any body of religious teachings.

THE GOSPEL OF THOMAS AND MYSTICISM

The recovery of humility toward Christian doctrine puts me in mind of a letter that John C. G. Wu wrote to Thomas Merton in 1961, encouraging him to pursue his interest in Taoist and Buddhist scriptures:

> The way to the re-Christianization of the post-Christian West lies through the East. Not that the East has anything really new to give the Gospel of Christ; but its natural wisdom is meant to remind Christians of their infinitely richer heritage, which, unfortunately, they are not aware of.[3]

The time has long passed since it became obvious that there are indeed things the East can give the Gospel of Christ. But the reminders have also been more than we might have expected. In the dialogue with the religions of the Far East, perhaps no part of that richer but neglected heritage has been more promising than the writings of the Christian mystics past and present. In many cases, it has been interest in the mystics on the part of those outside the Christian tradition that has led to a revival of interest among Christians eager to find common ground with Eastern religious ways. The role of mystical thought in the Christian theological tradition, where it is given a role to play at all, remains ancillary. Interest in the texts is primarily historical rather than formative. But in the meantime, mystical literature has figured prominently in the casting of new, multi-religious spiritualities in the West.

That familiarity with mystical thought softens the shock of the *Gospel of Thomas* to Christian sensitivities is hardly to be wondered at. In the same way that *Thomas* extends an open invitation to Buddhist reflections on Jesus and Christian reflections on the Buddha, it also insinuates new connections between Jesus' teachings and the marginal, and often doctrinally suspect, writings of the mystics. One of the clearest examples of such a connection is to be found in the sermons, legends, and proverbs of Meister Eckhart (1260–1328). Intersections of idiom and ideas are everywhere to be found, so much so that one has to suppose a parallel tradition transported from the first centuries right through to the High Middle Ages, like waters flowing beneath the surface of a river whose surface has frozen over.

Although Eckhart shares with the *Gospel of Thomas* the goals of reaching the place where religious ideas, images, beliefs, and practices are born, his strategy is different. *Thomas* takes an abstinent approach to religious language, using only a minimum of traditional vocabulary and even deliberately rejecting accepted usage. Eckhart, in contrast, takes as much as he can of the language of scripture in order to break through the words one by one, rendering transparent what is known in order to disclose what is unknown.[4] This gives added power to his insistence on a common birthplace for the divine and the human, a place that is at the ground of human interiority and yet is itself ungrounded. Eckhart invites us into a desert free of landmarks with which to orient ourselves toward the tradition we have left behind and detached from familiar language and conceptions, there to await the "little spark" of "uncreated light" that marks the "birth of God in the soul." *Thomas*, too, enjoins detachment from everything held sacred in order to lead us to the blinding light of the unborn in which the light of insight hidden with all images of divinity, humanity, and the world disappear into their source and out of sight. For both, only when the barrier between the interpreted and the interpreter collapses does one come to that place of life, that groundless ground where all things, just as they are, manifest a single human-divine-cosmic nature.

When we read Eckhart, we can only conclude that he would have understood the *Gospel of Thomas* from start to finish, without any sentiment of scandal and with no need to qualify Jesus' words:

> I have said before the shell must be broken through and what is inside must come out, for if you want to get at the kernel you must break the shell. And if you want to find nature unveiled, all likenesses must be shattered, and the further you penetrate, the nearer you will get to the essence. When the soul finds the One, where all is one, there she will remain in that One.[5]

Elsewhere, speaking of the vision that blinded Paul on the road to Damascus, Eckhart says:

> The light that is God flows out and darkens every light.... The light that is God is unmingled, no admixture comes in. This was a sign that it was the true light he saw, which is Nothing. By the light he meant quite simply that with his eyes open he saw nothing.... If the soul does not go out into external things, she has come home, and swells in her simple, pure light.... When the soul is blind and sees nothing else, she sees God.[6]

> For the more you empty yourself of yourself, the more you are master of yourself; the more you are master of yourself, the more you belong to yourself; and the more you belong to yourself, the more does God and everything he has created belong to you. In truth, I tell you: as true as it is to say that God is God and I am a man, if you were as empty of yourself as is the highest angel, the highest angel would belong to you, just as you belong to yourself. In this exercise one becomes master of oneself.[7]

Like *Thomas*, Eckhart frequently talks of letting go of images of God, since, as he says at one point, even the smallest image is as large as God himself, blocking it out like the smallest piece of dark paper placed in front of the eye blocks out the sun. Seeing through our images—or what Eckhart calls "seizing God in his robing-room"[8]—shows us the ineluctable duality of all knowing and in so doing brings us as close as we can to that point in self-knowledge where the duality is overcome. This is precisely what *Thomas* tries to do with its play of images and likenesses, to get at the heart of the religious dimension of the human by breaking through the religious dimension of conventional thinking:

> As long as you do works for the sake of heaven or God or eternal bliss, from without, you are at fault.... If a man thinks he will get more of God by meditation, by devotion, by ecstasies or by special infusion of grace than by the fireside or in the stable—that is nothing by taking God, wrapping a cloak around his head, and shoving Him under a bench. For whoever seeks God in a special way gets the way and misses God, who lies hidden in it.
>
> The least creaturely image that takes shape in you is as big as God. How is that? It deprives you of the whole of God. As soon as this image comes in, God has to leave with all His Godhead. But when the image goes out, God comes in.[9]

The similarities of thought and language are too many to reproduce in these pages, and here we have only touched on one of the many mystical writers that bear direct comparison to the standpoint of *Thomas'* Jesus. As impoverished as Christian doctrine would be without the humility and detachment to which mystical thought obliges us, our image of Jesus is no less impoverished without the Jesus that we meet in the *Gospel of Thomas*. Like Buddhist *upāya*, the mystical corrective reorients our search for literal beliefs to a search to see through the world of appearances, the only world we can know, to the only thing there is to see: the inborn desire to see itself. That giant among modern Christian mystics, Teilhard de Chardin, prefaced his study of human evolution with words that speak to the heart of the matter:

> *Seeing.* We might say that the whole of life lies in that verb—if not in end, at least in essence. Fuller being is closer union; such is the conclusion of this book. But let us emphasize the point: union can

only increase through an increase in consciousness, that is to say, in vision. And that, doubtless, is why the history of the living world can be summarized as the elaboration of ever more perfect eyes within a cosmos in which there is always something more to be seen.... To try to see more and better is not a matter of whim or curiosity or self-indulgence. *To see or to perish* is the very condition laid upon everything that makes up the universe.[10]

To stand where Teilhard stood to say what he said is the same place from which Eckhart and the living Jesus of the *Gospel of Thomas* stand. It is also the place from which we can begin to understand how much there is to learn from spiritual writings whose doctrine is so very different from our own. Far from providing just another stage to rehearse our respective prejudices, such dialogue helps expose our common neglect for the spirituality of the age and restore our enthusiasm for what lies beyond the frontiers of received tradition. Its assumption must always be that the truth of a religious heritage does not lie primarily in its texts and written documents, more or less badly executed in personal and institutional practices, but in the conversion of individuals who interpret those texts—and their praxis—in the light of the questions that the saeculum throws up to them. The point at which these questions not only oblige us to new ideas but collapse our certitudes and habits of thinking is the point at which the dialogue throws the past, naked but not ashamed, back into history.

CONCLUSIONS

The demands being made on contemporary Christianity around the world are unlike anything it has known in its long and varied history. They include adjustment to a diminished cultural role in traditionally Christian countries, to a religiously plural intellectual and spiritual environment, to an increasing variety of spiritualities among Christian believers and the felt need to appropriate the truth of other religious ways. While the Christian establishment cannot exercise control over the general historical background in which contemporary believers find themselves, it nonetheless is faced with the decision of where to draw the line between resistance and accommodation. Too much resistance risks alienating large numbers of Christians already embedded in some form of interaction with other religiosities; too little risks a loss of distinctive identity. As many Christians as there are who see the established churches as a guiding light, growing numbers see them as blocking out the light and casting a shadow over the search for understanding and religious experience.

It is hardly surprising—given this state of affairs—that the discovery in the mid-twentieth century of Christian texts lost since the early centuries of the church should excite the interest of those dissatisfied with the cautious if not intolerant response of the established churches to the spiritual movements of the age. Impatient to confirm their interest in ideas that have long foundered at the fringes of or under the surface of established Christian theology and catechesis, few take the trouble to follow the slow process of scholarly research on the conditions under which these texts were produced or to mistrust any but the most critical editions of the texts. The rediscovery of such texts is more than a matter for academic debate over their interpretation and how far they can be incorporated into the authoritative content of the tradition. It is, at least for some, a help to navigate their way as Christians in a religiously plural world. Whether this is perceived as a danger or an opportunity for the tradition as such in its present historical situation is largely a matter of whether one sees Christianity as enfolding the search for insight or the search for insight as enfolding

Christianity. To those who believe that the former is the case, these pages will, I am afraid, have offered little consolation.

Strategies focused only on shoring up Christianity against the black tide of non-Christian spiritualities seem doomed to irrelevance. The wiser course, and the course more in line with the history of the best that Christianity has had to offer through the centuries, is to reassess its spiritual resources for countering and encountering the ethos of the saeculum. Interest in things like in mystical literature and meditative practice has proved profitable for many as a way to open Christianity up to other religious ways. This interest in turn has created a receptivity to broadening the scriptural base of Christianity by studying and reflecting on the sacred texts of other traditions.

That said, there is still a sense in which the Christian fund of symbols, practices, and beliefs—and indeed *any* developed religious heritage—must seek to answer the whole of the human preoccupation with religion. Christianity matures in this task only in the measure that it expands its genius and history to the measure of what lies in the saeculum. And for that, it must rely in large measure on the elective spiritualities of the theologically unlettered. In a religiously plural world, the Christian church must learn to understand itself not only as the virgin mother of those who follow the teachings of Jesus, but as the child of its own children—in the words of the final Canto of Dante's *Divine commedia*, as "vergine madre, figlia del tuo figlio."

NOTES

1. VAN RUYSBEEK and MESSING 1993, 78.

2. John P. Meier, *A Marginal Jew: Rethinking the Historical Jesus* (New York: Doubleday, 1991, 1994), II, 426–7. Not surprisingly, Meier rejects outright any suggestion that the synoptic gospels draw from or depend on *Thomas* (476–7).

3. Letter dated Good Friday, 1961; quoted in Alexander Lipski, *Thomas Merton and Asia: His Quest for Utopia* (Kalamazoo, MI: Cistercian Publications, 1983), 11.

4. Bernard McGinn, *The Mystical Thought of Meister Eckhart: The Man from whom God Hid Nothing* (New York: Herder and Herder, 2001), 27. One cannot do better to understand Eckhart's strategy than to consult this remarkable work by a leading historian of the Christian mystical tradition.

5. Meister Eckhart, *Sermons and Treatises*, trans. by M. O'C. Walshe (Longmead: Element Books, 1987), II, 252 (Quint, Sermon 51).

6. *Sermons and Treatises*, I, 159–60 (Quint, Sermon 71).

7. From Amador VEGA ESQUERRA, *Maestro Eckhart: El fruto de la nada y otros escritos* (Madrid: Siruela, 1998), 144.

8. *Sermons and Treatises*, II, 118 (Quint, Sermon 40).

9. *Sermons and Treatises*, I, 118 (Quint, Sermon 5b).

10. Teilhard de Chardin, *The Phenomenon of Man* (New York: Harper Torchbooks, 1959), 31. We need to take care not to be detained so long in the *profanum* of the *Gospel of Thomas* that the sacredness of the text becomes subservient to the balance of scholarly opinion. To enter the *fanum* is to enter a different world. Not to recognize this is to risk the profanity of inoculating ourselves against being inspired by what we find there.

Bibliography

The following bibliography lists only works consulted in the interpretation of the logia of the *Gospel of Thomas*. Aside from other sources indicated in the introductory chapter, several of the volumes mentioned below include ample and up-to-date bibliographies of the scholarly work done on the *Gospel*. It seemed to me superfluous to reproduce that material here.

ARAI Sasagu 荒井 献
 1994 『トマスによる福音書』(Tokio: Kōdansha Gakujutsubunko).

BENTLEY, Layton, ed.
 1989 *Nag Hammadi Codex II, 2–7*. The Coptic Gnostic Library, vol. XX (Leiden: E. J. Brill).

CIVRA, Marco
 2001 *Il Quinto Vangelo e gli scritti attribuiti a Tomaso* (Torino: Marco Valerio Editore).

DAVIES, Stevan L.
 2005 *The Gospel of Thomas and Christian Wisdom* (New York: Seabury, 2nd edition).
 2002 *The Gospel of Thomas Annotated and Explained* (Woodstock, VT: Skylight Paths Publishing).

DECONICK, April D.
 2001 *Seek to See Him: Ascent and Vision Mysticism in the Gospel of Thomas* (Leiden: E. J. Brill).
 2006 *Recovering the Original Gospel of Thomas: A History of the Gospel and Its Growth* (London: T & T Clark).

DE SANTOS OTERO, Aurelio
 1999 "Evangelio de Tomás." *Los evangelios apócrifos* (Madrid: Biblioteca de Autores Cristianos), 678–705.

FRID, Bo, and Jesper SVARTVIK
 2004 *Thomasevangeliet med Jesusorden från Oxyrhynchus* (Malmö: Arcus).

FUNK, Robert W., Roy W. HOOVER, and the JESUS SEMINAR
    1997   *The Five Gospels: The Search for the Authentic Words of Jesus* (San Francisco: HarperSanFrancisco).

GÄRTNER, Bertil
    1961   *The Theology of the Gospel of Thomas* (London: Collins).

GRANT, Robert M. and David Noel FREEDMAN
    1960   *The Secret Sayings of Jesus according to the Gospel of Thomas* (London: Collins).

GUILLAUMONT, A., H. Ch. PUECH, G. QUSIPEL, et al.
    1959   *The Gospel of Thomas* (New York: Harper and Brothers).

KLOPPENBORG, John S., Marvin MEYER, Stephen J. PATTERSON, and Michael STEINHAUSER
    1990   *Q-Thomas Reader* (Sonoma, CA: Polebridge).

KOCH, Werner
    2003   *Du mein Bruder Thomas, sahst das Verborgene* (Rheinau: Drei Welten Verlag).

KOESTER, Helmut
    1990   *Ancient Christian Gospels: Their History and Development* (Philadelphia: Trinity Press International).

LAYTON, Bentley
    2004   *Coptic Gnostic Chrestomathy: A Selection of Coptic Texts with Grammatical Analysis and Glossary* (Leuven: Peters).

LELOUP, Jean-Yves
    2003   *Il Vangelo di Tommaso* (Roma: Edizioni Appunti di Viaggio).

MARKSCHIES, Christoph
    2002   *La Gnosis* (Barcelona: Herder Editorial).

MEYER, Marvin
    1992   *The Gospel of Thomas: The Hidden Sayings of Jesus* (San Francisco: HarperSanFrancisco).

MILLER, Robert J.
    1992   *The Complete Gospels* (Sonoma, CA: Polebridge Press).

PAGELS, Elaine
    2003   *Beyond Belief: The Secret Gospel of Thomas* (New York: Random House).

PATTERSON, Stephen J.
    1993   *The Gospel of Thomas and Jesus* (Sonoma, CA: Polebridge Press).
    1998   "Understanding the Gospel of Thomas Today," in PATTERSON et al., 1998, 33–75.

PATTERSON, Stephen, J. J. M. ROBINSON, H.-G. BETHGE
    1998   *The Fifth Gospel: The Gospel of Thomas Comes of Age* (Harrisburg, PA: Trinity Press International).

PERADEJORDI, Juli
2003   *Evangelio según Tomás: Las palabras secretas de Jesús* (Barcelona: Ediciones Obelisco).

PINCHERLE, Mario
2001   *Il quinto vangelo: Il vangelo di Tommaso con testo copto a fronte* (Diegaro di Cesena: Macro Edizione).

PIÑERO, Antonio, ed.
1997–   *Textos gnósticos. Biblioteca de Nag Hammadi* I (1997), II (1999),
2000   III (2000). (Madrid: Trotta).

RILEY, Gregory
1995   *Resurrection Reconsidered: Thomas and John in Controversy* (Philadelphia: Fortress).

ROBINSON, James M.
1990   (ed.). *The Nag Hammadi Library* (San Francisco: HarperSanFrancisco).
1998   "The Jesus of the Sayings Gospel Q," *Metanoia* 8, 1–2: 53–66.

TREVIJANO ECHEVERRÍA, Ramón
1997   *Estudios sobre el Evangelio de Tomás*. Fuentes Patrísticas, Estudios 2 (Madrid: Ciudad Nueva).

VALANTASIS, Richard
1999   *The Gospel of Thomas* (London and New York: Routledge).

VAN RUYSBEEK, Erik, and Marcel MESSING
1993   *Das Thomasevangelium: Seine östliche Spiritualität* (Düsseldorf: Patmos).

VIDAL MANZANARES, César
1991   *Los evangelios gnósticos* (Barcelona: Ediciones Martínez Roca).

WINTERHALTER, Robert
1988   *The Fifth Gospel: A Verse-by-Verse New Age Commentary on the Gospel of Thomas* (San Francisco: Harper & Row).

ZOCKLER, Thomas
1999   *Jesu Lehren im Thomasevangelium* (Brill: Leiden).

Text

These are the secret words that the living Jesus spoke and Didymos Judas Thomas wrote down.

1. And he said, "Whoever finds the meaning of these words will not taste death."

2. Jesus said, "Let those who seek not stop seeking until they find. When one finds, one will be troubled. When one is troubled, one will marvel and rule over all."

3. Jesus said, "If your leaders say to you, 'Look, the kingdom is in heaven,' then the birds will get there before you. If they say to you, 'It is in the sea,' then the fish will get there before you. Rather, the kingdom is within you and outside you. When you know yourselves, then you will be known, and you will understand that you are children of the living father. But if you do not know yourselves, then you are in poverty and you are poverty."

4. Jesus said, "The person old in his days will not hesitate to ask an infant of seven days about the place of life, and that person will live. For many who are first will be last, and will become a single one."

5. Jesus said, "Know what is in front of your face, and what is hidden from you will be disclosed to you. For there is nothing hidden that will not be manifest."

6. His disciples asked him, "Do you want us to fast? How should we pray? Should we give alms? What dietary regulations should we observe?"

Jesus said, "Do not lie, and do not do what you hate, because all things are revealed in the sight of heaven. For nothing is hidden that shall not be manifest, and nothing is covered that will remain undisclosed."

7. Jesus said, "Blessed is the lion that the human will eat, so that the lion becomes human; and cursed is the human that the lion will eat, and the lion will become human."

8. And he said, "The human being is like a sensible fisherman who threw his net into the sea. He drew it up from the sea and it was full of small fish. The fisherman found among them a fine large fish. He threw all the small fish back into the sea and chose the large fish without hesitation. Whoever has ears to hear, let them hear."

9. Jesus said, "Behold, the sower went out, took a handful of seeds, and scattered them. Some fell on the road and the birds came and pecked them up. Others fell on rock; they did not sink roots into the soil and produce heads of grain. Others fell among thorns; they choked the seeds and worms ate them. And others fell on good soil and produced good fruit—sixty measures and one hundred twenty measures."

10. Jesus said, "I have thrown fire on the world, and behold, I am watching over it until it blazes."

11. Jesus said, "This heaven will pass away and the heaven above it will pass away. The dead do not live and the living will not die. In the days when you ate what was dead, you made it alive. When you come into the light, what will you do? On the day when you were one, you became two. But when you have become two, what will you do?"

12. The disciples said to Jesus, "We know that you will be leaving us. Who will be our leader?"

Jesus said to them, "Wherever you are, you are to go to James the Just; heaven and earth came into being for his sake."

13. Jesus said to his disciples, "Compare me to something and tell who I am like."

Simon Peter said to him, "You are like a righteous angel."

Matthew said to him, "You are like a wise man."

Thomas said to him, "Master, my mouth is altogether incapable of saying what you are like."

Jesus said, "I am not your master. Because you have drunk, you are inebriated from the bubbling spring that I measured out."

And he took him and went aside and told him three things. When Thomas returned to his companions, they asked him, "What did Jesus say to you?"

Thomas said to them, "If I tell you one of the things he said to me, you will pick up stones and cast them at me. And fire will come out of the stones and consume you."

14. Jesus said to them, "If you fast, you will bring sin upon yourselves; and, if you pray, you will be condemned; and if you give alms, you will do harm to your spirits. When you enter a land and wander through the district, if people receive you, eat whatever they set before you. Heal the sick among them. For that which goes in your mouth will not defile you; it is what comes out of your mouth that will defile you."

15. Jesus said, "When you see one who was not born of woman, fall on your face and worship him. That one is your father."

16. Jesus said, "People might think I have come to cast peace on the world. They do not know that I have come to cast dissension on the earth: fire, sword, war. For there will be five in a house: three will be set against two and two against three, father against son and son against father, and they will stand alone."

17. Jesus said, "I will give you what no eye has seen, what no ear has heard and no hand has touched, what has never arisen in the human heart."

18. The disciples said to Jesus, "Tell us how our end will be."

Jesus said, "Have you found the beginning that you search for the end? For where the beginning is, there the end will be. Blessed is the one who will stand at the beginning. That one will know the end and will not taste death."

19. Jesus said, "Blessed is one who came into being before coming into being. If you become my disciples and listen to my words, these stones will serve you. For there are five trees in paradise that do not change in summer or winter and do not shed their leaves. Whoever knows them will not taste death."

20. The disciples said to Jesus, "Tell us, what is the kingdom of heaven like?"

He said to them, "It is like a mustard seed. It is the smallest of all seeds, but when it falls on plowed soil, it produces a great plant and becomes a shelter for the birds of the sky."

21. Mary said to Jesus, "What are your disciples like?"

He said, "They are like little children who have settled in a field that is not theirs. When the owners of the field come and say, 'Give us our field,' they undress before them in order to let them have their field back, and they return the field. Therefore I say, if the owner of a house knows that a thief is coming, he will stand watch before he arrives and will not let him break into his house of his estate and carry away his goods. As for you, be on your guard against the world. Arm yourselves with great strength lest the robbers find a way to get to you, for the trouble you expect will surely come.

"Let there be in your midst one who understands. When the crop ripened, he came quickly, sickle in hand, and harvested. Whoever has ears to hear, let them hear."

22. Jesus saw some infants nursing. He said to his disciples, "These nursing infants are like those who enter the kingdom."

They said to him, "Shall we then enter the kingdom as infants?"

Jesus said to them, "When you make the two one, when you make the inner as the outer and the outer as the inner and the upper as the lower, and when you make the male and the female into a single one, so that the male will not be male nor the female be female, when you make an eye in the place of an eye, a hand in the place of a hand, a foot in the place of a foot, and an image in the place of an image, then you will enter."

23. Jesus said, "I shall choose you, one from a thousand, and two from ten thousand, and they will stand as a single one."

24. His disciples said, "Show us the place where you are, for we must seek it."

He said to them, "Whoever has ears to hear, let them hear. There is light within a person of light and it lights up the whole world. When it does not shine, there is darkness."

25. Jesus said, "Love your brother like your soul; guard him like the apple of your eye."

26. Jesus said, "The chip that is in your brother's eye you see, but the log in your own eye you do not see. When you take the log out of your eye, then you will see to remove the chip from your brother's eye."

27. "If you do not fast from the world, you will not find the kingdom; if you do not keep the sabbath a sabbath, you will not see the father."

28. Jesus said, "I stood in the midst of the world and appeared to them in the flesh. I found them all drunk and none of them thirsting. My soul ached for the children of humanity, because they are blind in their hearts and do not see that they came empty into the world and seek to go out of the world

empty. But now they are drunk. When they have shaken off their wine, then they shall repent."

29. Jesus said, "If the flesh came into being because of spirit, it is a marvel; but if spirit came into existence because of the body, it is a marvel of marvels. Indeed, I am amazed at how such great wealth has made its home in such poverty."

30. Jesus said, "Where there are three gods, they are gods; where there are two or one, I am with that person."

31. Jesus said, "A prophet is not acceptable in the prophet's own village; a doctor does not heal those who know the doctor."

32. Jesus said, "A city built on a high mountain and fortified cannot fall, nor can it be hidden."

33. Jesus said, "What you hear in your ear, proclaim in the other ear from your housetops. For no one kindles a lamp and puts it under a basket, nor does one put it in a hidden place. One sets it on a lamp stand so that everyone who comes and goes will see its light."

34. Jesus said, "If a blind person leads a blind person, the two of them fall into a pit."

35. Jesus said, "It is impossible for one to enter the house of someone strong and take it by force without tying that person's hands. Then one can loot the house."

36. Jesus said, "Do not be anxious from morning to evening and from evening to morning about what you will wear."

37. His disciples said, "When will you be revealed to us and when will we see you?"

Jesus said, "When you undress without being ashamed, and you take your clothes and put them under your feet like little children and trample on them, then you will see the son of the living one and you will not be afraid."

38. Jesus said, "Many times you desired to hear these words I am saying to you, and you have no one else from whom to hear them. There will be days when you will seek me, and you will not find me."

39. Jesus said, "The Pharisees and the scribes have taken the keys of knowledge and hidden them. They did not enter themselves, nor have they allowed those who wish to enter to do so. As for you, be wise as serpents and as innocent as doves."

40. Jesus said, "A vine was planted outside of the father and did not grow strong. It will be pulled up by its roots and left to rot."

41. Jesus said, "Whoever who has something in hand will be given more; and whoever has nothing, even the little that person has will be taken away."

42. Jesus said, "Be passers-by."

43. His disciples said to him, "Who are you to say these things to us?"

"You do not know who I am from what I say to you but have become like the Jews. They either love the tree and hate the fruit, or they love the fruit and hate the tree."

44. Jesus said, "One who blasphemes the father will be forgiven, and one who blasphemes the son will be forgiven. But one who blasphemes the holy spirit will not be forgiven, either on earth or in heaven."

45. Jesus said, "Grapes are not harvested from thorns, nor figs from thistles, for these do not produce fruit. A good person brings forth good from the storehouse; a bad person brings forth evil from the evil storehouse of the heart and speaks evil things. Out of the abundance of the heart does such a person bring forth evil things."

46. Jesus said, "From Adam to John the Baptist, among those born of women, no one is so great as John the Baptist

that one's eyes should not be lowered in his presence. But I have said that whoever among you becomes a child will know the kingdom and will be greater than John."

47. Jesus said, "A person cannot mount two horses or stretch two bows. A servant cannot serve two masters without honoring the one and offending the other. No one drinks old wine and immediately wants to drink new wine. New wine is not poured into old wineskins lest they burst; and aged wine is not poured into new wineskins lest it spoil. An old patch is not sewn onto a new garment, because it would tear away."

48. Jesus said, "If two make peace between themselves in the same house, they shall say to the mountain, 'Move away,' and it will move."

49. Jesus said, "Blessed are the solitary and the chosen, because you will find the kingdom. For you have come from it and you will go there again."

50. Jesus said, "If they say to you, 'Where did you come from?' say to them, 'We have come from the light, from the place where the light came into being by itself, established itself, and reveals itself in their image.' If they say to you, 'Is it you?' say to them, 'We are its children and we are the chosen of the living father.' And if they ask you, 'What is the sign of your father in you?' say to them, 'It is movement and rest.'"

51. His disciples said to him, "When will the rest of the dead come about, and when will the new world come?"

He said to them, "What you look for has come, but you do not know it."

52. His disciples said to him, "Twenty-four prophets have spoken in Israel and they all spoke in you."

He said to them, "You have disregarded the living one who is before you and have begun to speak of the dead."

53. His disciples said to him, "Is circumcision beneficial or not?"

He said to them, "If it were beneficial, fathers would beget their children circumcised from their mothers. Rather, the true circumcision in spirit has become completely profitable."

54. Jesus said, "Blessed are the poor, for yours is the kingdom of heaven."

55. Jesus said, "Whoever who does not hate father and mother cannot be my disciple and whoever does not hate brothers and sisters and carry the cross as I do will not be worthy of me."

56. Jesus said, "Whoever has come to know the world has found a corpse; and whoever has found a corpse, the world is not worthy of that person."

57. Jesus said, "The kingdom of the father is like a man who had good seed. His enemy came at night and sowed weeds among the good seed. The man did not let them pull up the weeds but said to them, 'Do not go to pull up the weeds lest you pull up the wheat along with them.' For on the day of the harvest the weeds will be visible and will be pulled up and burned."

58. Jesus said, "Blessed is the one who has suffered and found life."

59. Jesus said, "Look for the living while you are alive, lest you die and then try to see him, and you will be unable to do so."

60. They saw a Samaritan trying to steal a lamb as he was going to Judea. He said to his disciples, "Why does he stalk the lamb?"

They said to him, "That he might kill it and eat it."

He said to them, "He will not eat it while it is alive but only after he has killed it and it has become a corpse."

They said, "Otherwise he could not."

He said to them, "You, too, seek a place for yourselves in rest, lest you become a corpse and get eaten."

61. Jesus said, "Two will be resting on a couch; one will die and one will live."

Salome said, "Who are you, sir, to come up on my couch and eat from my table?"

Jesus said to her, "I am he who is from the undivided. I was given some of the things of my father."

Salome replied, "I am your disciple."

Jesus said, "Therefore, I say, if one is undivided, one will be filled with light; but if one is divided, one will be filled with darkness."

62. Jesus said, "I tell my mysteries to those who are worthy of my mysteries. Do not let your left hand know what your right hand is doing."

63. Jesus said, "There was a rich man who had a great deal of money. He said, 'I will put my money to use so that I might sow and reap and plant and fill my warehouses with fruit, and thus be in need of nothing.' This was what he thought in his heart, but that very night he died. Whoever has ears, let them hear."

64. Jesus said, "A man had visitors and when he had prepared a banquet for them, he sent his servant to invite the guests.

"The servant went to the first and said, 'My master invites you.'

"That person said, 'Some merchants owe me money. They will come to me this evening; I must go and give them my orders. Please excuse me from the dinner.'

"He went to another and said to that person, 'My master invited you.'

"That person said to the servant, 'I have just bought a house and have been called away for the day. I will not have time.'

"He went to another and said, 'My master invites you.'

"That person said to the servant, 'My friend is going to be married and I am to prepare the dinner. I will not be able to come. Please excuse me from the dinner.'

"He went to another; he said to that one, 'My master invites you.'

"He said to him, 'I have bought a farm and am on my way to collect the rent. I will not be able to come. Please excuse me from the dinner.'

"The servant returned and said to his master, 'Those whom you invited to the dinner have asked to be excused.'

"The master said to his servant, 'Go out on the streets and bring back whomever you find so that they may dine.'

"Buyers and merchants will not enter the places of my father."

65. He said, "A good man had a vineyard. He leased it to some farmers so that they might work it and he might collect its produce from them. He sent his servant so that the farmers would give the servant the produce of the vineyard. They seized the servant, beat him, and almost killed him. The servant returned and told his master.

"His master said, 'Perhaps he did not know them.' He sent another servant. The farmers beat that one as well. Then the master sent his son and said, 'Perhaps they will respect my son.' Since the farmers knew he was the heir to the vineyard, they seized him and killed him. Whoever has ears, let them hear."

66. Jesus said, "Show me the stone that the builders rejected. That is the cornerstone."

67. Jesus said, "One who knows all things but is lacking in oneself lacks everything."

68. Jesus said, "Blessed are you when they hate you and persecute you. But they will find no place where they have persecuted you."

69. Jesus said, "Blessed are those who have been persecuted in their hearts. They are those who have truly come to know the father. Blessed are those who are hungry so that the belly of the one who hungers may be filled."

70. Jesus said, "If you bring forth what is within you, what you have will save you. If you do not have that within you, what you do have within you will kill you."

71. Jesus said, "I will destroy this house and no one will be able to build it."

72. A man said to him, "Tell my brothers to divide my father's possessions with me."

He said to him, "O man, who has made me a divider?"

He turned to his disciples and said, "I am not a divider, am I?"

73. Jesus said, "The harvest is great but the workers are few. So beseech the master to send workers to harvest."

74. He said, "Lord, there are many standing around the drinking trough, but there is nothing in the cistern."

75. Jesus said, "Many are standing at the door, but it is the solitary who will enter the bridal chamber."

76. Jesus said, "The kingdom of the father is like a merchant who had a supply of goods and discovered a pearl. The merchant was prudent. He sold the goods and bought the pearl alone for himself. You, too, must seek his treasure that does not perish, where no moth comes to devour and no worm destroys."

77. Jesus said, "I am the light that is above all things. I am all: all things came forth from me and all things have reached

me. Split a piece of wood; I am there. Lift up the stone and you will find me there."

78. Jesus said, "Why have you come out to the countryside? To see a reed shaken by the wind? And to see a man clothed in soft clothes like your kings and your great ones? They are dressed in soft clothes, and they are unable to understand the truth."

79. A woman in the crowd said to him, "Blessed are the womb that bore you and the breasts that nourished you."

He said to her, "Blessed are those who have heard the word of the father and have truly kept it. For there come days when you will say, 'Blessed are the womb that has not conceived and the breasts that have not given milk.'"

80. Jesus said, "Whoever has come to know the world has found the body, and whoever has found the body, the world is not worthy of that person."

81. Jesus said, "Let him who has become rich be king, and let him who possesses power renounce it."

82. Jesus said, "Whoever is near me is near the fire, and whoever is far from me is far from the kingdom."

83. Jesus said, "Images are visible to people, but the light within them is hidden in the image of the light of the father. He will reveal himself, but his image is hidden by his light."

84. Jesus said, "When you see your likeness, you rejoice. But when you see your images that came into being before you, that neither die nor become manifest, how much you will bear!"

85. Jesus said, "Adam came from great power and great wealth, but he was not worthy of you. For, if he had been worthy, he would not have tasted death."

86. Jesus said, "Foxes have holes and birds have nests, but the child of humanity has no place to lay his head and rest."

87. Jesus said, "Wretched is the body that depends on a body, and wretched the soul that depends on these two."

88. Jesus said, "Angels and prophets will come to you and give you what belongs to you. You, in turn, give to them what you have in your hands, and say to yourselves, 'When will they come and take what is theirs?'"

89. Jesus said, "Why do you wash the outside of the cup? Do you not understand that the one who made the inside is also the one who made the outside?"

90. Jesus said, "Come to me, for my yoke is easy and my lordship is gentle, and you will find rest for yourselves."

91. They said to him, "Tell us who you are so that we may believe in you."

He said to them, "You examine the face of the heavens and the earth, and yet you have not recognized the one who stands before you, nor do you know how to examine this moment."

92. Jesus said, "Seek and you will find. Those things you asked me about in the past, I did not tell you then. Now I am willing to tell you, but you do not seek them."

93. "Do not give what is holy to the dogs, or they will throw them on the dung heap. Do not throw pearls to swine, or they might [...] .

94. Jesus said, "One who searches will find, and one who knocks will be let in."

95. Jesus said, "If you have money, do not lend it at interest, but give to those from whom you will not get it back."

96. Jesus said, "The kingdom of the father is like a woman. She took a bit of leaven, hid it in dough, and made it into large loaves. Whoever has ears, let them hear."

97. Jesus said, "The kingdom of the father is like a woman carrying a jar full of meal. While she was walking along a distant road, the handle of the jar broke and the meal spilled out

behind her onto the road. She did not know it; she did not notice any problem. When she arrived at her house, she put the jar down and found it empty."

98. Jesus said, "The kingdom of the father is like a person who wanted to kill a powerful man. He drew his sword in his own house and thrust it into the wall to see if his hand would carry through. Then he killed the powerful one."

99. The disciples said to him, "Your brothers and your mother are standing outside."

He said to them, "Those here who do the will of my father, they are my brothers and mother. They are the ones who will enter the kingdom of my father."

100. They showed Jesus a gold coin and said to him, "Caesar's men demand taxes from us."

He said to them, "Give Caesar's things to Caesar; give God's things to God; and what is mine, give to me."

101. Jesus said, "Whoever does not hate his father and his mother as I do cannot be a disciple to me. And whoever does not love his father and his mother as I do cannot be a disciple to me. For my mother according to the flesh gave me death, but my true mother gave me life."

102. Jesus said, "Woe to the Pharisees, for they are like a dog lying in the cattle manger; it does not eat, nor does it let the cattle eat."

103. Jesus said, "Blessed is the man who knows where the robbers will enter, so that he will rise, gather his forces, and gird up his loins before they come in."

104. They said to him, "Come, let us pray today and let us fast."

Jesus said, "What sin have I committed? By what transgression have I been overcome? But after the bridegroom has left the bridal chamber, then let people fast and pray."

105. Jesus said, "One who knows one's father and mother will be called the child of a whore."

106. Jesus said, "When you make the two one, you will become children of humanity; and when you say, 'Mountain, move away,' it will move."

107. Jesus said, "The kingdom is like a shepherd who had a hundred sheep. One of them, the largest, wandered off. The shepherd left the ninety-nine and sought the one until he found it. After his toil he said to the sheep, 'I love you more than the ninety-nine.'"

108. Jesus said, "Whoever drinks from my mouth will become like me and I will become that person; and the things that are hidden will be revealed to that person."

109. Jesus said, "The kingdom is like a man who had a treasure hidden in his field but did not know it. When he died, he left it to his son. The son, not knowing of the treasure, took the field and sold it. The buyer went plowing and found the treasure. He began to lend money at interest to whomever he wished."

110. Jesus said, "Let whoever has found the world and become rich deny the world."

111. Jesus said, "The heavens and the earth will roll up in your presence, and whoever lives from the living one will not see death."

Does not Jesus say, "The world is not worthy of one who has found himself"?

112. Jesus said, "Woe to the flesh that depends on the soul; woe to the soul that depends on the flesh."

113. His disciples said to him, "When will the kingdom come?"

He said, "It will not come by expecting it to come. It will not be said, 'Look here' or 'Look there.' Rather, the kingdom of the father is spread out over the earth, and people do not see it."

114. Simon Peter said to them, "Let Mary leave us, for women are not worthy of life."

Jesus said, "Look, I will guide her to make her male, so that she, too, may become a living spirit resembling you males. For every woman who makes herself male will enter the kingdom of heaven."

The Gospel According to Thomas

You might also like . . .

James W. Heisig

Dialogues at One Inch Above the Ground
Reclamations of Belief in an Interreligious Age

Paperback, 224 pages, ISBN 978-0-8245-21141

James Heisig has spent his life traveling and learning from the philosophies and religions of the world while remaining a Roman Catholic. In this book, Heisig draws from these encounters to present invaluable insight into the interreligious age that is upon us.

> "Heisig writes with insight and depth, without soaring far in to the imagined skies of pretended concord and brotherhood and without cynically keeping his thought stuck in the mud. Rather, he, like his poet mentor Saigyō, moves just one small inch above our experienced lives—just enough to invite the reader to tread a little more lightly over this tattered earth."
>
> — John Keenan, author of *The Gospel of Mark: A Mahayana Reading*

Support your local bookstore or order directly from the publisher at
www.CrossroadPublishing.com

To request a catalog or inquire about quantity orders, please e-mail
sales@CrossroadPublishing.com

 The Crossroad Publishing Company

You might also like . . .

Raymund Schwager

Jesus of Nazareth
How He Understood His Life

Paperback, 192 pages, ISBN 978-0-8245-17113

This book takes a unique look at the life of Jesus and asks a
new question: How did Jesus himself come to understand life
and experience his faith? This imaginative narrative grounded
in scholarship suggests that powerful answer.

"A daring picture of a Jesus who has a real understanding of
what he is about. A gospel story emerges which nestles in,
and recasts, passages and themes from the Hebrew Scriptures. The result is the literary equivalent of a Fra Angelico
painting, full of gentle gravity and limpid light, a work
which both holds you still and beckons you onward."
— James Alison, author of
Raising Abel and *The Joy of Being Wrong*

Support your local bookstore or order directly from the publisher at
www.CrossroadPublishing.com

To request a catalog or inquire about quantity orders, please e-mail
sales@CrossroadPublishing.com

 The Crossroad Publishing Company

About the Author

James W. Heisig completed doctoral studies at Cambridge University, England, and lectured for several years in the United States and Latin America before joining the staff of the Nanzan Institute for Religion and Culture in Nagoya, Japan, in 1979 as a permanent fellow. During his years at the Institute, which he served as Institute director from 1991 to 2001, he has been actively engaged in promoting the dialogue among religions and philosophies East and West, both in Japan and throughout East Asia. His published books, translations, and edited volumes include some seventy-five titles in thirteen languages, among them *Imago Dei: A Study of C. G. Jung's Psychology of Religion* (1977), *Filósofos de la nada* (Barcelona, 2002), *Dialogues at One Inch Above the Ground* (2003), *Japanese Philosophy: A Sourcebook* (co-edited, 2011), and *Nothingness and Desire* (2013).

About the Publisher

The Crossroad Publishing Company publishes CROSS-ROAD and HERDER & HERDER books. We offer a 200-year global family tradition of books on spiritual living and religious thought. We promote reading as a time-tested discipline for focus and understanding. We help authors shape, clarify, write, and effectively promote their ideas. We select, edit, and distribute books. Our expertise and passion is to provide wholesome spiritual nourishment for heart, mind, and soul through the written word.